BATTLESHIPS, BUSES and BOMBERS

First published in 2009 by Middlesex University Press

Copyright © Jim Lewis

ISBN 978 1 904750 87 1

A CIP catalogue record for this book is available from The British Library

Design by Helen Taylor

Maps by Alice Gadney of Silver7 Mapping Ltd

Printed in the UK by Ashford Colour Press

Middlesex University Press
The Burroughs
Hendon
London NW4 4BT

Tel: +44 (0)20 8411 4162
Fax: +44 (0)20 8411 4167

www.mupress.co.uk

BATTLESHIPS, BUSES and BOMBERS

a history of transport
in the Lea Valley

Jim Lewis

Middlesex
University
PRESS

SPONSOR PROFILE

Middlesex University Press was supported in the publication of this book by the North London Strategic Alliance

The North London Strategic Alliance (NLSA) was established in 1999 as the sub-regional strategic partnership for North London, bringing together public, private and voluntary organisations, and covers the London boroughs of: Barnet, Hackney, Haringey, Enfield, Redbridge and Waltham Forest.

The aims of the NLSA are to:

- provide a sub regional voice for north London, via research and consultation, building consensus around the needs and opportunities of the sub-region, raising its profile and increasing public and private sector investment.

- promote the development of north London, encouraging and supporting partnerships across the public, private and voluntary sectors, to work together to benefit north London and London as a whole.

- act as ambassadors for the area, influencing key decision-makers and the development of policy in London and coordinating relationships between north London and regional and central Government.

DEDICATION

This book is dedicated to my family and also to
my late mother and father, Leonora Maud Lewis
and Walter Harry Portman Lewis.

ABOUT THE AUTHOR

Dr Jim Lewis has spent most of his career in the consumer electronics industry, apart from a three-year spell in the Royal Air Force servicing airborne and ground wireless communications equipment. When working in the Lea Valley for Thorn EMI Ferguson he represented the company abroad on several occasions and was involved in the exchange of manufacturing technology. Currently he is a Consultant to Terry Farrell & Partners on the historical development of London's Lea Valley and a Workers' Educational Association (WEA) tutor teaching industrial history. He also teaches students within the Community Programme who have learning difficulties. A freelance writer, researcher and broadcaster for his specialist subject – London's Lea Valley – he also has a genuine passion for encouraging partnership projects within the local community, which in the long term are planned to help stimulate social and economic regeneration. Dr Lewis is married with four grown-up children and lives in Lincolnshire.

The author Dr Jim Lewis cutting the ribbon, with the Director of the Pump House Steam & Transport Museum Trust, Lindsay Collier MA, to open a special exhibition commemorating the 90th anniversary of the birth of the Associated Equipment Company (AEC), Walthamstow, the company responsible for the founding of London Transport (now Transport for London). Lindsay Collier and the Pump House Steam & Transport Museum Trust are responsible for designing and promoting the *Lea Valley Experience* project.

SERIES ACKNOWLEDGEMENTS

The author wishes to thank the following organisations, companies and societies for their encouragement, support and advice and for supplying many of the illustrations within this book:

Alexandra Palace and Park Trust, Wood Green, London
BAE Systems, Farnborough, Hampshire
Bishopsgate Institute, London
Black & Ethnic Minority Business Association, Walthamstow, London
BOC Process Plants, Edmonton, London
Brooklands Museum, Weybridge, Surrey
Bruce Castle Museum, Tottenham, London
Civix, Exton Street, London
Corporation of Trinity House, Tower Hill, London
Cuffley Industrial Heritage Society, Cuffley, Hertfordshire
Edmonton Hundred Historical Society, Enfield, Middlesex
Enfield Archaeological Society, Enfield, Middlesex
Enfield Business Centre, Enfield, Middlesex
Enfield Energy Centre Limited, Enfield, Middlesex
Enfield Enterprise Agency, Enfield, Middlesex
Enfield Local History Unit, Enfield, Middlesex
English Heritage, Blandford Street, London
Epping Forest Museum, Waltham Abbey, Essex
Greater London Record Office, Northampton Road, London
Gunpowder Mills Study Group, Guildford, Surrey
Guy & Wright Ltd., Green Tye, Hertfordshire
Hackney Society, Hackney, London
Harper Collins Publishers, Hammersmith, London
Hawker Siddeley Power Transformers, Walthamstow, London
Historical Publications Ltd., Barnsbury, London
Hornsey Historical Society, Hornsey, London
House of Lords Record Office, Westminster, London
Imperial War Museum, Duxford, Cambridgeshire
Institution of Civil Engineers, George Street, London
Institution of Engineering and Technology, Savoy Place, London
Institution of Mechanical Engineers, Birdcage Walk, London
Jewish Museum, Finchley, London
John Higgs, Freelance Historian, Fairford, Gloucestershire
Johnson Matthey, Enfield, Middlesex
Lea Valley Growers Association, Cheshunt, Hertfordshire
Lee Valley Business and Innovation Centre, Enfield, Middlesex
Lee Valley Regional Park Authority, Enfield, Middlesex
London Borough of Enfield, Enfield, Middlesex
London Borough of Haringey, Haringey, London
London Borough of Newham, East Ham, London
London Borough of Waltham Forest, Walthamstow, London
London Lee Valley Partnership Limited, Great Eastern Street, London
London Organising Committee of the Olympic & Paralympic Games, Canary Wharf, London
London Waste Ltd, Edmonton, London
Lotus Engineering, Hethel, Norwich, Norfolk
Marconi Archive, Oxford University Library Services, Oxford, Oxfordshire

Markfield Beam Engine & Museum, Tottenham, London
Midland Publishing Limited, Earl Shilton, Leicester
Ministry of Defence Library, Royal Armouries, Leeds, Yorkshire
Museum of London, London Wall, London
National Archive, Kew, Richmond, Surrey
National Army Museum, Chelsea, London
National Maritime Museum, Greenwich, London
National Portrait Gallery, London
Natural History Museum, Kensington, London
Navtech Systems Ltd., Market Harborough, Leicestershire
New River Action Group, Hornsey, London
Newham Local History Library, Stratford, London
North London Strategic Alliance, Wood Green, London
Perkins Group, Leyton, London
Phillips Auctioneers & Valuers, New Bond Street, London
Potters Bar Historical Society, Potters Bar, Hertfordshire
Pump House Steam & Transport Museum, Walthamstow, London
RCHME Cambridge, (National Monuments Record), Cambridge, Cambridgeshire
Reuters Limited, Fleet Street, London
River Lea Tidal Mill Trust, Bromley-by-Bow, London
Royal Air Force Museum, Hendon, London
Royal Commission on Historic Manuscripts, Quality Court, Chancery Lane, London
Royal Society of Chemistry, Burlington House, London
Royal Television Society, Holborn Hall, London
Science Museum, Kensington, London
Scout Association, Chingford, Essex
Southgate District Civic Trust, Southgate, London
Speedway Museum, Broxbourne, Hertfordshire
Stratford City Challenge, Stratford, London
Tesco, Cheshunt, Hertfordshire
Thames Water, Reading, Berkshire
Thorn EMI Archive, Hayes, Middlesex
Tower Hamlets Local History Library, Tower Hamlets, London
University of Leicester Space Research Group, Leicester, Leicestershire
Upper Lee Valley Partnership, Tottenham Hale, London
Valley Grown Nurseries, Nazeing, Essex
Vauxhall Heritage, Luton, Bedfordshire
Eric Verdon-Roe, grandson of Alliott Verdon-Roe
Vestry House Museum, Walthamstow, London
Waltham Abbey Royal Gunpowder Mills Company Ltd., Waltham Abbey, Essex
Walthamstow Amateur Cine Video Club, Walthamstow, London
WEA, London District, Luke Street, London
Wordsworth Editions, Ware, Hertfordshire

While many individuals have freely given their knowledge, some unknowingly, which has contributed greatly to the production of this series of books, I have, on a number of occasions paid special tribute to certain people in the footnotes of various chapters.

I could not let the occasion pass without recording my sincere thanks to my wife Jenny for her superb editorial skills and outstanding patience. The author freely admits that this voluntary sacrifice on Jenny's part has comprehensively tested the cement that holds our wonderful marriage together.

AUTHOR'S NOTE

Events such as the Olympics can be brought into our homes and workplaces from the host country as they take place through the power of electronic communication – radio, television, the Internet and satellite broadcasts. The technology that allowed this to happen was first discovered and developed at Ponders End, Enfield in London's Lea Valley.

In November 1904, after much experiment, Professor Ambrose Fleming registered his patent for the diode valve, the world's first thermionic device. This inspired invention not only paved the way for today's multimedia electronics industry, but also created the delivery platform for space travel, e-mail and the Internet, not to mention computers.

Thirty-two years after Fleming's invention, in November 1936, the world's first high-definition public service television broadcasts were transmitted by the BBC from Alexandra Palace, positioned on the crest of the Lea Valley's western slopes.

Centring the 2012 Olympic and Paralympic Games in London's Lea Valley will provide a unique opportunity to remind the world that it was the development of electronic communication within the region that has allowed the participating nations to share the message of peace and friendship.

Jim Lewis

CONTENTS

INTRODUCTION

It is probably fair to say that authors who research interesting and little-known historical subjects tend to resist the requests of their readers to produce yet another book highlighting new facts. Then, as in my case, the pressure becomes too great and the research bullet has to be bitten. Once the decision is made there is no turning back and the author is faced with months, sometimes years, of archive research to follow up reader leads and to see if sufficient material exists in a particular subject area to construct an interesting and worthwhile story. While the prospect of the challenge at first may appear daunting, once fully committed and immersed in the work the excitement level builds and it is particularly satisfying when new information comes to light.

In my last three books, I invited readers, particularly teachers and school children, to get involved in Lea Valley projects and also to take on the role of detectives to discover if more interesting stories existed about the region. Some schools and universities rose to the challenge and on a number of occasions I was invited to become involved and also to act as a Lea Valley tour guide. It is occasions like these that make writing doubly rewarding.

Due to considerable local interest, and also the requests by many retailers for reprints of earlier material, the author has been persuaded to deviate from the intentions of the original format used in my earlier Lea Valley books, that of keeping chapters deliberately short, and for this new series I shall include a fuller treatment of many of the subjects. Therefore, it is intended to give each book in the series a particular theme. In this way it is hoped that that the readers' requests will be largely satisfied and also a greater insight into the developments of the region will be achieved.

I have been greatly encouraged to be quoted by prominent writers and broadcasters such as Ian Sinclair and also to receive letters from Dr Adam Hart-Davis saying "I had no idea that the great George Parker Bidder was, no less, 'the maker of modern West Ham'. I told the story in the wilds of Moretonhampstead."The BBC newscaster Mike Embly, once referred to me as the "Lea Valley alarm clock" as

I appear to wake people up to the historic significance of the region. These compliments make the long hours in front of a computer screen and the many years of archive research seem worthwhile and this encourages me to discover and write more about the Lea Valley, its entrepreneurs and its world firsts. Perhaps, sometime in the future the region will no longer be Britain's best-kept secret.

As I am mindful that the forthcoming Olympics will bring many people to the Lea Valley from around the world, who will want to learn a little more about the region, I have decided to include some stories to attract those readers with broader interests beyond that of the subject of industrial heritage.

Jim Lewis

1. LONDON'S TRANSPORT LEGACY

The nineteenth century was an age of great change and much innovation as inventors, engineers and entrepreneurs came together to meet the challenges created by man's quest for better living standards. Huge strides were made locally, particularly in the technical development of mass transport and long-distance communication. There were also major advances in the discovery and development of several new materials. Once these particular materials were introduced into the manufacturing process they would bring about a revolution that would have a huge impact on the development of our modern world.

The legacy of the early visionaries – who constantly struggled to solve difficult problems, often before the appropriate technology became available – must be viewed from today's perspective as a truly remarkable feat of perseverance. In many instances the dedication and ingenuity shown by these people has added much to our knowledge and shaped the way that we think, live, work and play.

When we think of the manufacture of road vehicles in this country our thoughts are usually drawn to the midland area of England and perhaps other regions such as the north west and north east. Here, particularly in the periods before and following the Second World War, large numbers of commercial and domestic vehicles were produced, although in recent years there has been a rapid decline in the number of indigenous British manufacturers.

Latterly, due to new investment by overseas producers, with interests in increasing their share of the European market, there has been a revival of motor vehicle manufacturing in Britain. However, it is perhaps fair to say that seldom do we consider that London, and in particular the Lea Valley, was at one time a region which accommodated different generations of inventors and entrepreneurs who were responsible for much of the early development of road transport in Britain.

WALTER HANCOCK

From the late eighteenth century, men like Richard Trevithick and others had experimented with different types of steam transport, but it was not until the 1820s that engineers began in earnest to tackle the many practical problems of moving people by road. It would therefore seem reasonable to speculate that the interest of this later group had been stimulated by the experiments of those other engineers, like George Stephenson, who were developing the means to move people and goods by rail.

One of the earliest British engineers who had ideas of moving people en masse by road was Walter Hancock (1799-1852). Born at Marlborough, Wiltshire, Hancock served an apprenticeship to a London watchmaker and jeweller. It would appear, however, that Hancock had set his sights on heavier things for, in about 1824, he set up an engineering works in the east end of London, on the south side of Stratford High Street. Between 1824 and 1836, Hancock carried out experiments to demonstrate the practicality and also the advantages of employing steam carriages on common London roads.

Walter Hancock (1799–1852).

Hancock had wisely concluded that vehicles travelling over the somewhat questionable road surfaces of the day would present him with a greater number of engineering problems to overcome than had been encountered by those engineers who were developing steam engines to run on smooth rails. Early on he had realised that it was crucial for road vehicles to be made as lightweight as possible to reduce the risks of mechanical damage and also of suffering the embarrassment of becoming bogged down in potholes. He had also wanted to ensure that any future public transport system that was based on road vehicles was safe, economical and reliable. Hancock, perhaps more than any other of his inventor peers, had appreciated that the safe transportation of passengers was fundamental to any design consideration so that public confidence in such a revolutionary method of travel could be quickly gained. Probably his biggest engineering task was to ensure that steam, contained under high pressure in close proximity to passengers, would not, in extreme circumstances, prove hazardous to a travelling public.

In the past, steam engine designers had developed thick-walled metal pressure vessels to contain the steam and to work a piston and cylinder system connected to a crank. This type of arrangement

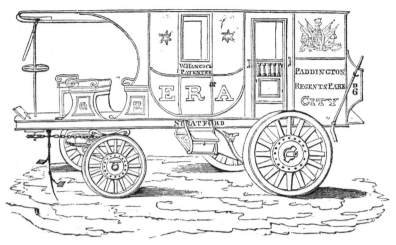

A drawing of Walter Hancock's steam road coach *Era* built at Stratford in east London in 1834.

was both heavy and bulky and if the pressure vessel exploded – which occasionally it was apt to do – the flying pieces of metal could prove fatal to anyone nearby. Hancock overcame the majority of these problems by designing a lightweight, coke-fired engine that did not have a piston or cylinder. He also solved the explosive properties of the pressure vessel by designing a unique system that was devoid of metal. In Hancock's words: "it has two flexible steam receivers, which are composed of several layers of canvas, firmly united together by coatings of dissolved caoutchouc or India rubber, and are thus enabled to resist a pressure of steam of sixty pounds upon the square inch". The arrangement can be likened to a pair of bellows that inflate and deflate alternately, having a similar action to a cylinder and piston. Interestingly, India rubber and like materials would turn out to play an important part in Hancock's future career.

Over a period of about fifteen years Hancock produced a number of novel steam carriage designs which he tested and modified, using the practical experience he had gained by driving them around the streets of London and further afield, under all manner of conditions. He appears to have given up on his India rubber-coated pressure vessel quite early in his experimental programme, perhaps because the material became unreliable as improved vehicle designs called for increased steam pressures. However, Hancock never gave up on the notion of passenger safety and greater efficiency. By the late 1820s he had abandoned his experiments of trying to improve the working of conventional water tube boilers (those which relied on hot gases from the fire-box rising and heating the water in a system of pipes) for his own invention, the safer and more efficient "chamber boiler". This he patented in 1827 and it became recognised as one of the most powerful and safest of light boilers to be used in steam carriages.

The first steam-powered vehicle Hancock developed was a three-wheeled, four-seater car which was probably one of the first dedicated to moving people by road in Britain. In 1832 Hancock built another road vehicle, the *Era*, for the London and Brighton Steam Carriage Company. Hancock's fame appears to have spread, as in April the following year the London and Paddington Steam Carriage Company launched a service with his steam road coach, *Enterprise*, a vehicle which was capable of carrying fourteen passengers. By October 1833 another of Hancock's vehicles, the *Autopsy*, ran a limited service between London's Finsbury Square and Paddington, and in October the following year he introduced the *Erin* which ran between the City and Paddington.

As might be imagined, and as with most new schemes or inventions, there were those, usually from amongst the traditionalists,

The *Enterprise*, constructed in 1833 at Stratford in east London by Walter Hancock. This vehicle was capable of carrying fourteen people.

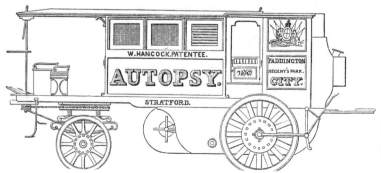

A drawing of Walter Hancock's steam road coach *Autopsy* built at Stratford in east London in 1833.

A drawing of Walter Hancock's steam road coach *Automaton* built at Stratford in east London in 1836.

competitors, and horse omnibus operators and drivers who complained, criticised and physically obstructed Hancock when he drove his carriages through London's busy streets. Apart from the general range of grumbles about the vehicles' excess speed, noise and ability to scare horses, many thought that it would be impossible for Hancock's steam carriage to ascend steep hills. In true Hancock fashion (he was good at taking on his critics through articles and in the letter columns of the press) a challenge was laid down to the traditional horse-drawn transport users to see who would be the first up Pentonville Hill (a London road between Kings Cross railway station and the Angel public house in Islington), a slope that was calculated to have a rise of one in eighteen to twenty. On the day of the challenge Hancock reported:

> a severe frost succeeding a shower of sleet, had completely glazed the road, so that horses could scarcely keep their footing. The trial was made, therefore, under the most unfavourable circumstances possible; so much so, that, confident as the writer felt in the powers of the engine, his heart inclined to fail him. The carriage, however, did its duty nobly. Without the aid of propellers, or any other such appendage, [then generally thought necessary even on a level road] the hill was ascended at considerable speed, and its summit successfully attained, while his competitors with their horses were yet but a little way from the bottom of the hill.

There is no doubt that Hancock, for his day, was successful in advancing the technology of steam-powered road transport. One of his later projects was a vehicle, the *Automaton*, capable of carrying twenty-two passengers at a top speed of twenty miles per hour. Although Hancock had been relatively successful with his road carriage designs, particularly with the *Era, Infant, Erin* and *Enterprise* – which had been run by him and others, carrying many thousands of passengers on commercial routes – the days of steam carriage transport were fairly short lived. In 1840 the Turnpike Acts were being enforced in London and heavy tolls were levied on mechanically propelled vehicles, severely penalising operators using this type of transport. It would also appear that about this time the public had lost interest in the novelty of steam road transport. Because of these unfavourable circumstances, the companies that had invested in the new technology floundered through lack of revenue. Hancock's business was also affected by these events. However, Walter Hancock's engineering and entrepreneurial skills were soon about to be extended in an entirely different direction.

By the early 1840s Hancock had turned his energies to working with his brother Thomas who had premises in Goswell Road, London. It is not clear if, at that time, Walter appreciated the connection his move would make between his former experiments with road transport and the future discoveries of his brother.

Between 1820 and 1847, Thomas Hancock had taken out sixteen patents relating to successful developments in the processing of India rubber. His discoveries were of such significance that they were used by the now famous Charles Macintosh & Co., originally of Glasgow, in the preparation of waterproof garments. Hancock eventually became a partner in the firm although he still carried on with his business in London.

Perhaps even more importantly, Hancock was able to demonstrate that India rubber, which became brittle when cold and sticky when hot, could be made stable against wide variations of temperature by the application of sulphur. On 21st November 1843 he patented a process based upon his discovery which was effectively an early form of vulcanising. Whether coincidence or not, this discovery would seem to place both men on the road transport pioneering rostrum.

However, in America Charles Goodyear, remembered for his association with vehicle tyres, had been working on a similar method of vulcanising for a number of years although he did not patent his process until 1844. Goodyear filed a legal suit against Hancock for allegedly stealing his idea, but he subsequently lost the case.

GUTTA PERCHA – WHAT IS IT?

Towards the end of 1843, samples of gutta percha had been sent to this country from Singapore in the hope that experimenters could discover useful ways of using the material (gutta percha is a leathery substance that is derived from the latex of certain trees that grow in the Far East and South America and, although similar, it has a different molecular structure from that of rubber). It so happened that Hancock's younger brother Charles, an artist by profession, had been sent a sample of the material and after much experiment, he registered, on 15th May 1844, a patent for "improvements in cork and other stoppers and a new composition… employing a vegetable extract, introduced from the East Indies, but never before made use of… in the arts and manufactures of this country, called gutta percha".

In late 1844 or early 1845 a Dublin chemist, Henry Bewley, who had wanted to manufacture soda water and was having difficulties containing the gaseous liquid, had become interested in Charles Hancock's patents for making bottle stoppers. On 4th February 1845 Charles and Henry Bewley signed an agreement to develop Charles's patent for their joint benefit and eventually, around 1846, they were to form the Gutta Percha Company, probably to carry out experimental work. The company was thought to have been established somewhere in Stratford High Street, east London, although the exact location has yet to be established. However, there is a reference to "a large shed beside the horse-pond at Stratford Essex, [being] rented for twenty pounds a year" (of course, with further research, this could turn out to be the High Street address). Samuel Gurney, the prominent Quaker banker, arranged financial backing for the embryonic venture and Walter Hancock joined the company.

The India Rubber & Gutta Percha & Telegraph Company in Silvertown, east London. In 1864 S.W. Silver, a company that had its roots in the eighteenth century, took over the business of Charles Hancock. Previously Charles had jointly taken out a patent with Stephen Silver (junior) for waterproofing and insulating materials.

Not long after the establishment of the Gutta Percha Company at Stratford, Henry Bewley took on a financial partner by the name of Reynolds and soon afterwards a larger factory was taken at 18 Wharf Road, Islington. Here, with the injection of new capital, modern machinery was installed and a consultant engineer appointed. It would therefore seem clear from this initiative that opportunities had been spotted by the partners, which led them to

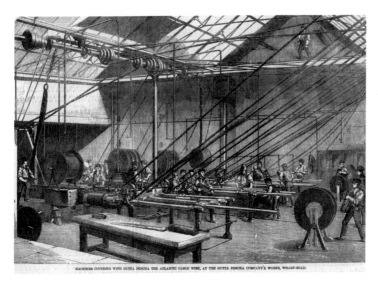

MACHINES COVERING WITH GUTTA PERCHA THE ATLANTIC CABLE WIRE, AT THE GUTTA PERCHA COMPANY'S WORKS, WHARF-ROAD.

A view of gutta percha wire-covering machinery at a factory in Wharf Road, Islington. It is interesting to note that on 29th July 1848 Charles Hancock had registered a patent for a "Wire Covering Machine".

believe that it would be advantageous to be in at the start of a new and potentially lucrative market that was beginning to develop for gutta percha products. Many uses for the new material would be found, including the manufacture of soles for boots and shoes, which were reported to be harder wearing than leather.

Michael Faraday, the celebrated electrical engineer and developer of the dynamo, had suggested that the material would be excellent for covering telegraph cables (the first submarine cable to be laid was beneath the English Channel between Dover and Calais in 1851). Faraday had discovered that when gutta percha was purified and processed by Charles Hancock's methods, it became an excellent electrical insulator. It was probably this particular property that had led Faraday to conclude that the material would be suitable for under-water use.

On 29th July 1848, after much experiment and with the assistance of one of his sons and brother Walter, Charles was able to register a patent for a "Wire Covering Machine" that could cover a continuous length of wire with gutta percha. Charles Hancock's invention was to herald the start of a new industry that would bulk-manufacture subterranean and submarine cables, insulated with the material, the processing methods of which he had pioneered.

FREDERICK BREMER
The next significant milestone in Lea Valley road transport began in a small workshop, more like a shed, in the back garden of a house in Connaught Road, Walthamstow in east London.

Frederick Bremer was born on 12th July 1872 in Mile End Road, east London the fourth son of a German boot maker Gerhard Bremer and his wife Lydia. Frederick was one of nine children, having five brothers and three sisters. In 1888 the family moved to Connaught Road, Walthamstow, the place where Frederick would develop his engineering skills. There, between 1892 and 1894, Frederick Bremer built the first British car to be powered by an internal combustion engine.

Fortunately for the technically minded, in 1974 the staff and students of the former Barking College of Technology were able to produce drawings, a report and probably the following technical description of the workings of the car. For readers with a mild tendency to nod off to sleep during detailed technical mechanical explanations, it is recommended that the following indented paragraphs are skipped!

> The engine is a single cylinder horizontal bore 3 5/16" stroke 5 3/16" water jacket and cylinder liner. The head water jacket and cast-iron liner are held in position by four studs screwed in the bedplate and tightened by nuts on the head. The flywheel is balanced. The engine is fitted with half compression for starting and is automatically changed to full compressing by lifting a trigger on the cam rocker, a spring pushing the rocker over. The small spring on the trigger is for keeping the trigger in the slot in the cam rocker spindle. The inlet valve is automatic, and the exhaust valve tappet is adjustable. Under the dome of the induction pipe there is fitted a small valve. The engine is lubricated by wick and drip feed lubricators. The cylinder and piston are lubricated by a lubricator placed on top of the cylinder, the oil passing through the cylinder to the piston, thence round and through the piston to the gudgeon pin bush in the connecting rod when the piston reaches the bottom of the stroke. The big-end is lubricated by wick lubricator, the main bearings by drip feed lubricators.

> Ignition is by trembler coil and wipe contact, and is variable.

> The carburettor is fitted with a cork float and is adjustable for petrol level, the

Frederick Bremer (1872–1941).

Frederick Bremer, c.1893, and the car he built in his workshop behind his mother's house in Connaught Road, Walthamstow.

vaporising chamber is fitted with wicks and is water heated by means of a false bottom to the vaporiser. A mixture regulator is fitted, and means are provided for air to pass through the petrol to replace the vapour drawn off, and by turning the mixture regulator the amount of air is varied in proportion to vapour. The amount of gas to the engine is regulated by a throttle fitted to the induction pipe and extra air is admitted to the engine at high speed by a small valve fitted under the dome of the engine. The carburettor has been reconstructed owing to damage by fire.

The engine is water cooled, the water being carried in tanks placed on each side of the body.

The car is driven by means of crossed belts from flywheel pulleys to fast and loose pulleys on the countershaft, then by chains to sprockets on the rear wheels. The centre pulley is fitted with a differential gear and transmits the power to the rear wheels, the other pulleys running loose. The speeds are obtained by sliding one of the belts from a loose pulley to the centre pulley, the other belt running idle, the sliding or striking operation being operated by two levers on the dash board. (One set of striking gears is missing.) Owing to the different diameters of the pulleys on the flywheel, fast and slow speeds are obtained by the sliding belts.

The countershaft is adjustable by means of two bolts fitted to each bearing. It will be noticed that the holes on the brackets are

A 1974 drawing by C. Watkins of the complete Bremer car with upholstered seat and front-mounted petrol tank.

radial slots so that the countershaft can be for distance from the rear axel for the purpose of tightening chains or belts. The brake is by hand lever operating on the spoon brakes on each tyre (the foot gear is missing). The sub axles swivel on centre pivots on the front axel, the steering is differential and is operated by a tiller arm on the dash board, the tiller being adjustable for height by sliding up and down the column. The petrol tank (missing) was fitted to the front of the dash board (replica now in place).

The Bremer car on a lorry c.1918. On the left of the picture is Frederick Bremer and to the right is Tom Bates, his assistant.

In December 1894 the car had its first road trials in skeleton form, the body being added in January the following year.

There does not appear to have been any attempt to put the car into production – Bremer seems to have built the vehicle by way of a personal challenge. After a period of virtual neglect in a garden shed, Bremer offered the car to Vestry House Museum, Walthamstow, where it was placed on show in 1931. In 1962 the car was withdrawn from display so that restoration work could be carried out and in the autumn of the following year the vehicle's engine was coaxed into life.

The car was entered in the London to Brighton Veteran Car Run in November 1964 and broke down after completing seventeen miles when the crankshaft failed. In the following year it travelled the full fifty-four miles in seven hours and fifty-five minutes, consuming three gallons of petrol, half a gallon of oil and twelve gallons of water. Frederick Bremer's car was returned to the Vestry House Museum where it remains on permanent display.

The restored Bremer car in the specially built gallery at the Vestry House Museum, Walthamstow.

Frederick Bremer died in 1941 and was buried in St Mary's churchyard, Walthamstow along with his wife Annie. Sadly their

The Frederick Bremer School, completed in 2008; a fitting memorial to Walthamstow's automobile pioneer.

grave has become overgrown but the memory lives on in the name of the Frederick Bremer School, opened in September 2008 and dedicated to the teaching of engineering. The new school replaces two former Walthamstow schools, Warwick School for Boys and the Aveling Park School.

AEC – THE FORERUNNER OF LONDON TRANSPORT (NOW TRANSPORT FOR LONDON)

The next phase in the Lea Valley road transport story began with the unlikely intervention of Arthur Salisbury-Jones, a member of the Stock Exchange. Salisbury-Jones had hit on the idea of starting a large scale motor-bus company to serve London's commuters, which if successful he would expand to cover the whole of Britain. In January 1905 he launched the London Motor Omnibus Company which proved to be so successful that other bus companies were quickly introduced to the metropolis. By the middle of 1907, Salisbury-Jones had over three hundred passenger-carrying vehicles on London's roads.

At the outset, Salisbury-Jones had recognised that to achieve his aims and objectives he would need to control closely the manufacture and design of his vehicles. This he did by forming the Motor Omnibus Construction Company in February 1905 and in August the following year a small tin hut was rented in Hookers Lane, Walthamstow. Initially parts were purchased from a range of outside contractors to be assembled into vehicles. However, by January 1907 a new 30,000-square-foot factory was opened at Hookers Lane which brought in house much of the work provided previously by the outside suppliers. By the following year the factory had doubled in size and the workforce had increased from the original six in 1906 to over five hundred and seventy.

The rapid expansion of the London transport system had caused vehicles to be purchased from a range of sources, many coming from overseas. Naturally the lack of standardisation caused a number of problems for the embryonic transport service, with vehicle safety and reliability featuring high on the list. In 1906 alone it is recorded that London buses were involved in 2,448 accidents, many of these attributed to mechanical failure.

The rate of expansion had placed Salisbury-Jones and the other major bus operators in financial difficulties and it was clear that swift action needed to be taken or the whole operation would fail. In 1908 it was therefore decided to restructure the companies through a merger and this was achieved by joining with the London General Omnibus Company (LGOC), an organisation which had

originally been founded in 1855 to consolidate and regulate the multitude of horse-drawn bus operators that were plying their trade on the streets of the capital. Other operators that formed the amalgamation were the "Vanguard" and "Union Jack" fleets. This now provided the basis for vehicle standardisation and improvements in reliability and design. Out of the amalgamation, in October 1910, came the creation and introduction of the now famous B-type bus, which superseded the X-type.

Further structural changes took place in June 1912 when the vehicle construction side of the London General Omnibus Company was hived off to form the now more familiar Associated Equipment Company Limited (AEC). This was achieved when the Underground Electric Railways Company (UERC) took control. At the time (UERC) owned most of the London Underground system and also a large proportion of the London tramway network.

The restructuring had brought about improved efficiency and economies of scale which saw output of the B-type increase from around three per week in October 1910 to fifty per week in March

An early AEC B-type bus, c.1914, of the London General Omnibus Company, built in Walthamstow. The bus ran on the 35 route from Leyton to the Elephant and Castle. Note the advertisements for Warner flats to rent, from 5s/6d (27.5p) to 10s/6d (52.5p) per week.

An aerial view of the AEC factory which once stood at the junction of Blackhorse Lane and Forest Road, Walthamstow (now the car park for Blackhorse Road underground station). The company moved to Southall, Middlesex in 1928.

1913. In this year, there were over 2,000 B-types on the road and their reliability was such that collectively, for every 100,000 miles travelled, there were only fourteen unscheduled stops.

With the coming of the Great War (1914–18) there was a need to turn Britain's factories over to the production of military equipment and in 1916 the government took control of the Walthamstow AEC factory. From then until the end of the War the factory turned out approximately nine hundred buses that were sent to the front to support the movement of troops. The initial need by the military for transport was so great that the first buses sent to the front were unmodified and still in their "general" livery. The later versions were painted khaki and had their windows removed and replaced with wooden planks. Some B-types were converted to mobile pigeon lofts so that carrier pigeons, part of the early wartime communication system, could be safely housed. Others became mobile anti-aircraft gun platforms. When the War ended, the B-types were used to ferry the thousands of troops home.

We all owe a great debt of gratitude to these early road transport pioneers, and in particular to the vision and initiative of Arthur Salisbury-Jones, who laid the foundation of London Transport, now Transport for London.

The unmistakable AEC badge that, over the years, adorned thousands of their vehicles.

In 1928 AEC moved from Walthamstow to a new factory site at Windmill Lane, Southall, Middlesex, ending its association with the Lea Valley.

REFERENCES

Author unknown, *London Transport Museum*, London Transport Museum, 1980.

Author unknown, "Development of the Bus in London", *Modern Transport*, 7, 14 January, 18 February 1956.

Author unknown, *The Bremer Car - Its History & Technical Description,* London Borough of Waltham Forest Libraries & the Arts Department, Waltham Forest, c.1974.

Author unknown, *The Telcon Story,* The Telegraph Construction & Maintenance Company Limited, 1950.

Baldwin, Nick, "AEC - The Early Years", *The Vintage Commercial Vehicle Magazine,* Vol.3, No.9, July/August 1987.

Belmont, James, "Centenary of Hancock's Steam Carriage", *The India-Rubber Journal,* 30th May 1936.

Day, John R., *The Story of the London Bus*, L.T. Publications, London, 1973.

Dennis, John A., "AEC - 50 Years", *AEC Gazette*, November/December 1962.

Hancock, Walter, *Narrative of Twelve Years' Experiments (1824-1836),* John Weal, Architectural Library, London, 1838.

Hancock, Walter, "Charles Hancock - Artist and Inventor", *Chemistry and Industry*, 30th September 1950.

Karwatka, Dennis, *Technology's Past*, Prakken Publications Inc., Kentucky, 1995.

Lee, Sidney (ed.), *Dictionary of National Biography*, Smith Elder & Co., 1909.

Lewis, Jim, *East Ham & West Ham Past*, Historical Publications Ltd., 2004.

Powell, W.R. (ed.), *The Victoria History of the County of Essex,* Vol.6, Oxford University Press, Oxford 1973.

Thomson, L.A., *By Bus Coach and Tram in Walthamstow,* Walthamstow Antiquarian Society, London, 1971.

Townsin, Alan, "The Way it was at AEC", *The Vintage Commercial Vehicle Magazine,* Vol.4, No.18, January/February 1989.

White, William, *Gazetteer and Directory of Essex*, Robert Leader, Sheffield, 1848.

2. THE EAST END ENGINE BUILDERS

Stratford in east London has witnessed the birth and development of a diverse range of industries from the making of artistic porcelain to the less attractive production of paint and chemicals with its pungent aromas. The establishment of the locomotive and carriage works of the Great Eastern Railway, based at Stratford, also allowed generations of train spotters to indulge their hobby.

In 1848, the Eastern Counties Railway, as it was then known, moved its main locomotive workshops from Romford in Essex to a site in London's east end – located north of Stratford High Street. It would appear that the Northern & Eastern Railway had already established a small repair shop at Stratford as early as 1839 and it was this facility which the Eastern Counties Railway leased in January 1844, perhaps with a view to the move in 1847–8 in mind. However, at the time, it is doubtful if the consolidation of the maintenance facility would be seen by those early planners as starting a process which was to alter radically the social and economic face of Stratford for over a hundred years. From a site of about fifteen acres and a workforce of a few hundred around the middle of the nineteenth century, the facility had grown to seventy-eight acres and employed over six thousand by the early part of the twentieth century. By the 1920s the area occupied by the Great Eastern

A view of the general offices of the Great Eastern Railway Works, Stratford, east London, c.1920, after alterations had taken place. Note the design of the weathervane.

The Drawing Office of the Great Eastern Railway Works, Stratford, east London, c.1920.

Railway, as it had become known in 1863, had almost doubled to approximately one hundred and thirty-three acres. This included the adjacent wagon building and repair facility at Temple Mills.

The move to Stratford not only brought the construction of new buildings, which would eventually lead to the carrying out of just about every type of rolling stock repair imaginable, but also the building of three hundred homes to house the workforce and their families. Soon the district became known locally as "Hudson's Town" after the railway entrepreneur, George Hudson. As late as the 1950s the area was referred to as the "New Town" by residents with long memories or those with railway connections. Even today, names like Waddington Road and Waddington Street (after Hudson's traffic manager) remind us of the area's railway heritage.

Over the years, the railway works at Stratford were home to several notable engineers and superintendents who were responsible for the introduction of many new ideas and much technical innovation. In 1850, under John Viret Gooch, the works completed their first railway engine. This suggests a major change of direction for the company, as it would have required a considerable amount of capital investment to complete such a venture. At the time, it must have been obvious to those responsible that once tooling up for engine building had begun, there would be a need for ongoing investment in plant and machinery as the future technology of railway engines and other rolling stock changed. Also, it will be remembered that the Stratford works was heavily committed to providing a maintenance and repair service for the Great Eastern Railway which, in the years to come, would no doubt become more complex as the amount of rolling stock in circulation increased.

An engine under construction at the Great Eastern Railway Works, Stratford, east London.

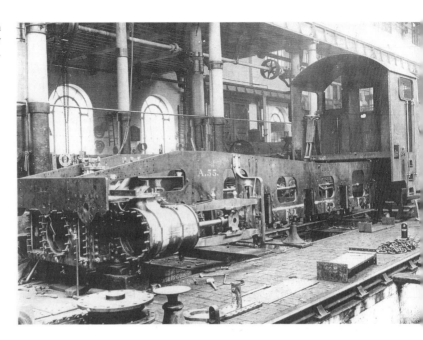

However, it would appear that the decision to build railway engines was successful, as construction lasted at Stratford up until the 1920s. During this period, 1,682 locomotives were built along with some 5,500 passenger vehicles and in excess of 33,000 goods wagons. This would equate to a complete engine being turned out every two weeks over a period of seventy years – a remarkable achievement.

Other remarkable achievements occurred, particularly when Stratford was under the superintendence of James Holden, when the works responded to a number of engineering challenges. In February 1888 the Crewe works of the London North Western Railway had built a locomotive in 25.5 hours. This record was

A first-class railway carriage after being upholstered at the Great Eastern Railway Works, Stratford, east London.

quickly eclipsed in America by June the same year, at the Altoona works of the Pennsylvania Railway, when the time was lowered to 16.5 hours. The challenge was taken up by the Stratford works when, in December 1891, the time for construction was brought down to 9 hours and 47 minutes – a world record for this class of engine. This record was never beaten.

James Holden, in bowler hat, superintendent of the Great Eastern Railway Works, Stratford, east London, standing with crew and railway workers in front of a 0-4-4 engine c.1897.

The construction time included applying a single coat of protective grey paint to both engine and tender before the locomotive left the works for trials. In the case of the two previous records the engines had to be returned to their respective works for painting directly after completing their initial trials. The Stratford engine (0-6-0 small-boilered freight type) was put into regular service hauling coal and had covered some 36,000 miles before being returned to the works for painting. Following 43 years of service she was scrapped in January 1935 after covering the remarkable distance of 1,127,750 miles.

In the late 1880s the management of the Stratford works received complaints that they were polluting the River Lea. This had come about through a discharge of oil from the site. At the time the works operated an oil-gas plant to manufacture fuel for the lights in the company's carriages and it was the waste from this process which had leaked, or perhaps been deliberately discharged, which had caused the problem.

The Decapod (0-10-0) railway engine c.1902. Although Holden was responsible for the engineering development of this engine, much of the Decapod's design was completed by the talented railway engineer Fred Russell.

Holden addressed the problem and, after carrying out a number of experiments, he came up with an inspirational idea. His solution was to design a system which would burn the unwanted oil waste as a supplement to coal in the fireboxes of converted engines. The first of these conversions (2-4-0, class T19) in 1893 carried 500 gallons of oil in a tank fitted to the tender. Later versions could carry 650 gallons. In all, around 60 such engines were converted to burn oil and it would appear that they did so until the supplies of the waste product ran out. It was then considered uneconomic to continue running these engines by bringing in alternative oil supplies.

By the turn of the century electric motive power was beginning to challenge steam as the new energy source. This gave designers the ability to build engines which could accelerate rapidly. Once again James Holden's engineering skills were put to the test to see if steam could remain competitive. His answer, in 1902, was to design the Decapod (the first 0-10-0 in Britain) which could attain 30mph in 30 seconds from a standing start pulling a train of 300 tons tare weight. Although at the time it was claimed that the Decapod was

The Decapod under construction at the Great Eastern Railway Works, Stratford, east London.

The Robin Hood (4-6-0) being prepared at Stratford for an exhibition at Southend, Essex in 1956. After Nationalisation in 1948 the Works lost its Great Eastern Railway title and became part of British Railways.

Engine No. 930 (0-6-0), which was built in the world-record time of 9 hours and 47 minutes over two days, 10th and 11th December 1891, at the Great Eastern Railway Works, Stratford, east London.

The Claud Hamilton, one of several express (4-4-0) engines built at the Great Eastern Railway Works, Stratford, east London.

A photograph of the eighty-five workmen who were responsible for building Engine No. 930 (0-6-0) in world-record time. The engine was also given a coat of grey paint before it began trials.

the most powerful locomotive in the world, it was never put into regular service in its original form as the rate of acceleration was thought too severe for the bridges and track.

By January 1923 the Great Eastern Railway had merged with five other railway companies to form the London and North Eastern Railway (LNER) and it was shortly after this amalgamation that the decision was taken to cease building new rolling stock at Stratford.

When the railways were nationalised in 1948, the Stratford works continued its locomotive repair role under British Rail. However, by the 1950s and 1960s new technology, in the form of electric and diesel locomotives, was being introduced as the railway networks pushed forward with programmes of modernisation. These measures were to have serious consequences for the Stratford works. Gradually departments closed and sections of the site were redeveloped to handle international freight transport. Nevertheless, a much-reduced repair facility remained until 1991, when in March of that year the works finally closed, ending a proud chapter of London's east end industrial history. The 151 years of railway engineering activity, between 1840 and 1991, are thought to represent a world record for continuous locomotive repair on one site.

STRATFORD'S RAILWAY CONNECTIONS LIVE ON AS A REGENERATION STRATEGY

Stratford's geographic position, in the lower Lea Valley, has made the London Borough of Newham into Britain's new railway hub, allowing the continuation of one hundred and seventy years of railway history. The ground formerly occupied by the Great Eastern Railway Works has now become part of a complex infrastructure which joins together, through the new Stratford International Station, the Channel Tunnel Rail Link (CTRL), the London

Underground Network, Docklands Light Railway (DLR) and National Rail overground services. Furthermore, the Crossrail funding agreement – announced in December 2008 by Andrew Adonis, Transport Minister, Boris Johnson, Mayor of London and Sir Michael Snyder, head of policy at the City of London Corporation – has guaranteed Newham a liberal share of London's regeneration cake. Responding to the announcement, Sir Robin Wales, the Mayor of Newham commented, "This is really good news for Newham. Crossrail will mean not just quicker and less crowded journeys for residents to central London, it will also vastly improve accessibility to the borough's key development sites at Stratford and the Royal Docks, stimulating greater investment and creating thousands of additional jobs and homes".

The busy concourse in front of Stratford International Station.

At the northern extremity of Newham is a region known as Temple Mills where, in October 2007, a vast new regeneration project was completed that has established an important link to the future and also a connection with Stratford's railway past. The project referred to is Eurostar's £400 million rolling stock maintenance depot. A state-of-the-art depot, housed in a building approximately 450 metres long by 64 metres wide, that can cope with the complexities of servicing trains that are designed to run on both the British and continental rail networks. While passengers are silently whisked through the Kent countryside, under the

Stratford International Station under construction.

The newly constructed (2008) Temple Mills Eurostar maintenance depot.

Inside the Temple Mills Eurostar maintenance depot with carriages on elevated tracks.

A radio-controlled battery-powered shunter used for moving rolling stock at the Temple Mills maintenance depot.

Last remaining building of the Great Eastern Railway Works, Stratford being used by the channel tunnel contractors for storage (2000).

English Channel and onward through France and Belgium at speeds of up to 186mph, they are totally unaware of the train's ability to cope with the three different power sources and its onboard capability to operate with up to seven different signalling systems.

Inside the depot shed, eight 400-metre tracks allow complete trains to be serviced without the necessity of uncoupling and thereby causing costly delays. Previously trains had to be broken into two sections to accommodate the smaller maintenance shed at the former North Pole depot in west London (interestingly, the name North Pole is taken from a nearby road). Here, the broken-up units

Eurostar at Stratford International Station: photograph by Andrew Baker.

had to be shunted into their respective positions so essential maintenance work could be carried out; then after servicing the process was reversed to unite both halves once more.

Many practical lessons were learned from the way the former North Pole depot handled rolling stock and this has translated into dramatic improvements in the maintenance facilities and the lay-out at Temple Mills. For example, a bi-directional carriage washing plant, toilet-emptying facilities to handle two trains, and a system to monitor the condition of wheels automatically, have been implemented. Temple Mills also boasts a unique system for personal safety for maintenance staff working on trains that can be powered by 1.5kV (kilovolts), 3kV and 25kV. Power to the system can be controlled and also personnel monitored through an electronic arrangement of smart card and personal identification numbers (PINs).

It would be interesting to observe the reactions of the late James Holden if it were possible for him to see Temple Mills today.

REFERENCES

Aldrich, Langley, C., *The Locomotives of the Great Eastern Railway - 1862-1962*, C. Langley Aldrich, Essex 1969.

Allen, Cecil, J., *The Great Eastern Railway*, Ian Allan, London, 1976.

Author unknown, "Memoranda connected with the Locomotive and Carriage Works at Stratford and the Wagon Works at Temple Mills", Great Eastern Railway, London, June 1921.

Farmer, Jack, *The Great Eastern Railway as I Knew It*, J.R. Farmer, Theydon Bois 1990.

Gordon, W.J., *Our Home Railways - The Great Eastern Railway, Vol. 1*, Frederick Warne & Co., London, 1910.

Grantham, Andrew, "Depot mark 2 promises faster maintenance of faster trains", *Railway Gazette*, October 2007.

Hawkins, Chris and Reeve, George, *Great Eastern Railway, Part One - Stratford, Peterborough & Norwich Districts*, Wild Swan Publications Ltd, Oxford, 1986.

Pember, Geoffrey, Gr*eat Eastern Railway 0-4-4 Tank Locomotives*, Great Eastern Railway Society, London, 1979.

Sainsbury, Frank, *West Ham 1886-1986*, Council of the London Borough of Newham, London 1986.

Note

There is a giveaway in the name Temple Mills that provides a clue to the site's historic origins. The name comes from a time when the area was associated with the Knights Templar, an order said to have begun around 1118 after the

First Crusade. In 1185 the Knights were granted land, in the region now known as the lower Lea Valley, by William of Hastings, steward to Henry II. Here they built water mills for the grinding of grain and seed. The order was dissolved in 1312 by Pope Clement V.

3. A.V. ROE – THE LEA VALLEY FLYER

The engineer and aviator Edwin Alliott Verdon-Roe (he preferred to be called Alliott) was born on 26th April 1877 at Patricroft near Manchester. He first became interested in flight while serving in the Merchant Navy. On a voyage in 1902 he watched a soaring albatross which afterwards inspired him to build and experiment with a variety of model aircraft, some of which he displayed at the 1906 and 1907 Motor and Aeronautical Shows which were held in the Agricultural Hall, Westminster, London.

Alliott Verdon-Roe (1877–1958).

As interest in aviation grew in Britain, Lord Northcliffe of the *Daily Mail* newspaper offered cash prizes for models weighing between two and fifty pounds (1–22kg) capable of flying above the height of fifty feet (15.2m). In 1907 Roe won the highest awarded prize of £75 for the flight of his nine foot six inch (2.85m) wing-span model in a competition held at the Alexandra Palace in Wood Green, north London. Although the amount of money was meagre, in relation to supporting future experimental and development work, the prize won by Roe's rubber powered entry no doubt helped to encourage him to pursue his ambitious plans.

In 1908 Roe formed his first serious business partnership with the now famous Tottenham engineer J.A. Prestwich with capital of £100, but their J.A.P. Avroplane Company was short lived, lasting a little over one year. It has been suggested that the reasons for failure of the partnership were the

The A.V. Roe triplane, powered by a J.A.P. engine, gets airborne over Walthamstow marshes c.1909.

repeated interruptions by police of test flights. These were for "causing a disturbance" when aircraft flew over the Lea Marshes at between four and five o'clock in the morning. There has also been another suggestion that Roe and Prestwich parted amicably as neither could agree the dimensions for a new triplane design. Perhaps we shall never know the real reason.

To raise the finance required for further development and experimentation, Roe borrowed from both his father and brother Humphrey. The latter owned a factory in Manchester manufacturing elasticated trouser braces under the trade name Bulls Eye. In gratitude for the financial support given by his brother, Roe displayed the name Bulls Eye on his triplane (this was probably one of the first flying advertisements in the world). A partnership with Humphrey culminated in the formation, in 1910, of the now more familiar A.V. Roe and Company.

Under the new partnership arrangements Humphrey (who was to later marry Marie Stopes, the prominent campaigner for women's rights and founder of Britain's first family planning clinic in north London) took responsibility for all matters of finance and management, allowing Alliott to concentrate his engineering skills on aircraft design and development. However, it would appear that under this new arrangement Humphrey wanted much closer control of operations, so a workshop facility was established in the factory of Evershead & Co. at Ancoats, Manchester, which allowed him to keep a close rein on the business. The arrangement saw aircraft, built in Manchester, transported south for flight testing at Brooklands, Surrey.

Roe built his first full-size biplane in 1907, but could not complete tests until the end of that year. He had chosen the Brooklands race-track for his experiments, as it turned out not a particularly wise move as officialdom insisted that he placed the workshop – a wooden shed 40 feet by 20 feet (12.2m x 6.1m) – that would house his plane, all in one place, alongside the finishing straight. This meant that he had to wait until the racing season finished before commencing serious trials. There were also other bureaucratic restrictions which did not allow Roe to sleep in his workshop and this would restrict his chances of preparing the aircraft for early morning flights when the air was still. However, he seems to have overcome this particular obstacle by developing the habit, when leaving each evening, of greeting the gate-keeper with a cheery "good night" and then a little later scaling the perimeter fence to gain entry to the site undetected.

The 6hp J.A.P. engine used in the first trials was not sufficiently powerful to get Roe airborne and he therefore resorted to borrowing a 24hp Antoinette engine from the French manufacturer, Levasseur. With this, and after much modification to the wings and airscrews, he was able to make a few successful hops. Financial pressures saw the return of the Levasseur engine to its maker and eviction from the Brooklands site. Roe was offered only £15 by the Brooklands management for his workshop, which he reluctantly accepted and went to live with his brother, Dr Verdon-Roe in Putney who allowed him to build his next aircraft, a triplane, in his stables.

A.V. Roe at the controls of his triplane (1909) on Walthamstow marshes. Note that the aircraft is not covered in fabric.

In his search for a suitable testing ground, Roe's attention finally turned towards the Lea Valley where the Great Eastern Railway had established a new spur line in 1840. Roe was able to rent two arches, in 1909, underneath the brick viaduct on Walthamstow Marshes which took the railway across the River Lea to its destination at North Chingford. The accommodation was ideally placed to allow rapid flight testing of aircraft after construction, necessary repairs or modification, although the surrounding marsh was not wholly suitable for the take off and landing of Roe's fragile machine. It was reported that the ground near the arches was "dotted about with stumps of wood to which donkeys and goats were tethered". Roe's initial flights were said to be "a 50-yard hop, a crash and then two weeks' work".

The A.V. Roe triplane (1909) on Walthamstow marshes. In the background can be seen the Liverpool Street to Chingford railway viaduct across the River Lea. Roe used the arches for his workshop.

However, despite the various logistical and other problems, it was from this particular site, on 13th July 1909, that A.V. Roe made his historic flight in a triplane, powered by a 9hp J.A.P. engine. This was not only an all-British first but a double first for the Lea Valley, as the engine was manufactured close by in the works of J.A. Prestwich (J.A.P.) at Tottenham, adding another chapter to the list of technological achievements for the region. A blue English Heritage plaque, placed on the viaduct wall adjacent to the railway arches where the plane was housed and prepared, now marks the location of A.V. Roe's flight.

For a number of years there has been considerable confusion over claims concerning who made the first powered flight in Britain in an all-British aircraft and the actual location where this occurred.

On 16th October 1908, almost five years after the Wright brothers, Wilbur and Orville, made their epic flight at Kitty Hawk, North Carolina, USA, S.F. Cody, an American, made the first official flight in Britain in British Army Aeroplane No.1. He covered a distance of 1,390 feet (423.7m). J.T.C Moore-Brabazon, a Briton, flew 1,500 feet (457.2m) in a French Voisin on 2nd May 1909. In neither of these flights can it be claimed that it was an all-British aircraft with a British-made engine and a British pilot.

When Roe was still at Brooklands he took a biplane off the ground on 8th June 1908 achieving several hops of two to three feet above

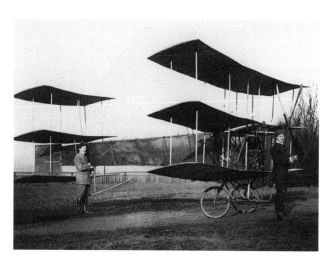

The triplane on Lea Marshes with A.V. Roe standing by the propeller.

the race track. However, Roe did not make these early flights known until some two years later. The Gorrell Committee of the Royal Aero Club, in 1928–9, disallowed A.V. Roe's claim to having been the first to fly in Britain on the grounds that he had not flown for a sufficient distance. They ruled that Moore-Brabazon was the first genuine Briton in the French aircraft.

Nevertheless, A.V. Roe's flight from Walthamstow Marshes on 13th July 1909, when he flew about 100 feet (30.5m) in his triplane, was the first official flight of an all-British aircraft with a British pilot. On 23rd July 1909, Roe extended the flight distance to 900 feet (274.3m) at an average height of 10 feet (3.04m).

Roe was a practical man, always looking for ways to simplify aircraft design and in particular making them easier to fly. He pioneered many methods of streamlining and simplifying, not just the obvious parts of an aircraft, but structural airframe components. In 1906 he was the first engineer in the world to develop, and patent, a design to combine both lateral and elevator control in a single steering column. This innovation allowed pilots to fly an aircraft more easily than by the previous cumbersome, two-lever control system. Early in 1912, although this time not in the Lea Valley, Roe claimed a

A tight squeeze! A.V. Roe poses with his biplane inside his workshop/aircraft hanger at Brooklands.

further success, when his company built and flew the first aeroplane in the world with an enclosed cockpit.

During his lifetime, Roe and his company designed, developed and manufactured many successful aircraft. In 1913, with the stirrings of the Great War (1914-18) clearly on the horizon, A.V. Roe & Co. came up with one of their most innovative and reliable designs, the Avro 504. The aircraft entered military service with the Royal Flying Corps (RFC)

The A.V. Roe stand (centre of picture) at Olympia, London 1910.

and the Royal Naval Air Service (RNAS). The aircraft's design allowed it to perform many different roles from gun spotting to pilot training. November 1914 saw the Avro 504 carry out a successful bombing raid on the Zeppelin sheds at Friedrichshafen. When the Royal Air Force (RAF) was formed in 1918, the Avro 504 continued in service up until the early part of World War Two.

After the Great War, as might be imagined, orders for military aircraft were drastically reduced and company finances suffered. Although there had been major investments by Manchester industrialists, by 1928 Roe had sold his interest in A.V. Roe & Co. to Sir John Siddeley, the head of Sir W.G. Armstrong-Whitworth & Co, Ltd. Alliott then

An Avro Lancaster (c.1943) of the famous 617 ("Dambusters") squadron which has been adapted to carry the Barnes Wallis bouncing bomb. The explosive for the bomb (RDX) was developed at part of the Royal Gunpowder Mills complex at Waltham Abbey, Essex.

A restored Avro 504 in flight. This aircraft became the backbone of the Royal Flying Corps during the First World War and continued in service with the Royal Air Force up until the beginning of the Second World War.

left and bought an interest in S.E. Saunders Ltd., a manufacturer of flying boats at Cowes on the Isle of Wight, the company becoming Saunders-Roe Ltd. Perhaps the move indicated that Alliott was looking for another challenge, in the field of flying boat design. As early as 1913 he had built a 100hp seaplane which was sufficiently advanced to interest the British Admiralty. Alliott was knighted in 1929 for his services to the aircraft industry and up until his death at the age of eighty, on 4th January 1958, he remained the president of Saunders-Roe.

We in the modern world owe a great debt of gratitude to the vision, determination and resourcefulness of these early pioneers. It is impossible to say how slow technical progress might have been if these visionaries had not had the drive and perseverance to secure the necessary finances to turn their dreams into reality.

A.V. Roe in his study in 1954 at the aged of seventy-seven when he was still president of Saunders-Roe.

REFERENCES

Author unknown, *An Air Pioneer in Walthamstow*, Occasional Publication No.15, Walthamstow Antiquarian Society.

Jackson, A.J., *Avro Aircraft Since 1908,* Putnam Aeronautical Books, 1965, revised and updated by R.T. Jackson, 1990.

Ludovoci, L.J., *The Challenging Sky: The Life of Sir Alliott Verdon-Roe,* Herbert Jenkins, London, 1956.

Verdon-Roe, Eric, (grandson of A.V. Roe), private conversation and correspondence, January 2008.

Who Was Who (1851–1960), Oxford University Press.

Note

The company founded by A.V. Roe designed and manufactured the aircraft that helped Britain and her Allies secure the peace in the two World Wars. But, between 1941 and 1943 A.V. Roe lost two of his sons – Eric and Lighton – who were killed in action. Both were Squadron Leaders, serving with the RAF and RAF Volunteer Reserve respectively.

4. J.A. PRESTWICH – TOTTENHAM'S PROLIFIC INVENTOR

John Alfred Prestwich was born on 1st September 1874 in Kensington, London. The family appears to have moved to Warmington House in Tottenham High Road a little before the boy's fourteenth birthday. Here John's father continued his business as a photographer, which probably explains why the boy took an early interest in moving picture technology, which at the time was at an early stage of development.

At school young Prestwich is said to have acquired a good understanding of mathematics and draughtsmanship which gained him two scholarships, one to the City and Guilds School and the other to the City of London School. It is also said that he showed an

John Alfred Prestwich (1874–1952), founder of the company.

early aptitude for things mechanical, building his first model steam engine by the age of fourteen. On leaving school at the age of sixteen, Prestwick went to work for the Ferranti company, which at the time was producing electrical equipment and scientific instruments at a premises located at Aldgate in the east end of London. By the age of eighteen, Prestwich had moved to a firm which was engaged in the manufacture of a range of heavy engineering work, from locomotives to wood-carving machines.

However, it would seem that Prestwich was unable to contain his enthusiasm for developing his own ideas and in 1895, at the age of twenty, he set up on his own account as the Prestwich Manufacturing Company, making electrical fittings and scientific instruments, in a greenhouse at his parents' Tottenham home.

As the moving picture craze hit Britain in the late nineteenth century, Prestwich was able to put his earlier photographic knowledge together with his considerable engineering skills to produce a range of equipment for the burgeoning industry.

From early sales brochures it can be seen that Prestwich's output was prolific. He invented, designed and manufactured cameras, printers and projectors as well as machines for perforating, measuring and cutting film. He also became expert at the art of making and showing films. This no doubt got the young man noticed, as for a brief period he entered into partnership with the man sometimes credited with inventing the cinematograph, William Friese-Greene. On 21st June 1889, Friese-Greene had filed his patent, No.10,131, for "a camera for producing a series of photographic images in rapid succession upon a celluloid film".

Although Prestwich continued with his photographic business for almost twenty years, he was unable to resist his first real love – that of designing and making engines. Prior to his marriage in 1898 to Elinor Bramley, he had acquired No.1, Lansdowne Road, Tottenham for his workshop and he now took up residence next door, at No.3, with his new bride.

A Prestwich motion picture camera on Captain Scott's Antarctic Expedition of 1910. The cameraman is Scott's official expedition photographer, Herbert Ponting.

W.H.PRESTWICH.F.R.P.S

A J.A. Prestwich No. 7 projector complete with lantern and swing-out base. It would appear that this picture was taken at the Lansdowne Road works as the inside of the large workshop doors can be seen in the background.

A page from a Prestwich trade catalogue advertising the patent Kinematograph camera, model No.4, c.1900.

THE . .
5

"Prestwich" Patent Kinematograph Camera.
MODEL 4

This instrument is now so well known and used by so many of the well-known film makers, that any commendatory remarks are unnecessary.

The " claw " or " pin " movement is entirely different from any other on the market, and has never been equalled for accuracy, simplicity and durability.

This camera being very simple, better results are obtained by those of little experience.

POINTS—The registration or spacing of the film is absolutely accurate.

The system of magazine change boxes, which are fitted to the camera render it very convenient; the standard sizes contain 400 to 500 feet of film (according to thickness), which may be exposed in short lengths on different subjects. An indicator is fitted to the camera for showing the quantity (in feet) of film used, the number being discernible while the machine is being operated.

The camera is very small and compact, weighs only 8½ lbs., and when packed in case with magazines is as portable as a half-plate outfit.

If desired it can be carried in a square travelling case, with the film boxes fixed ready for exposure. In this form the travelling case is rather larger than when the film boxes are carried detached, but is as compact and convenient as any other make with self-contained boxes carrying only 170 feet of film.

The spacing of the pictures is absolutely accurate at all speeds. The accuracy of the spacing does not depend on any gears cams, or delicate parts, and the accuracy is not impaired by constant use.

All parts are beautifully made, the best gun metal and steel being used in construction, and case is of polished mahogany.

The mechanism being fitted to a solid brass angle plate prevents any warping. The camera is therefore well suited for use in tropical climates.

Used on most of the Scientific expeditions and by the principal film makers throughout the World.

Constructed on an entirely original principal.

Weighs only 8½ lbs.

Perfect Registration.

Simplicity of Working.

Every Instrument Guaranteed.

Beautifully Compact.

Perfection in Workmanship.

Improved in Detail.

	£	s.	d.
" Prestwich " Patent Kinematograph Camera, with 2 Magazines for 400 to 500 feet of film	35	0	0
Tripod, best polished ash, very rigid	1	10	0
Extra Magazines of brass bound polished mahogany for 500 feet	1	15	0
Large View Finder, with Lens and Ground Glass	0	18	6
Dallmeyer Special Stigmatic Lens, 3 in. focus, full aperture f/5 and special hood	4	0	0
Dallmeyer ,, 2 in. focus, full aperture f/4 and special hood	3	0	0
Leather Bound Canvas Case for Camera, Magazines and Accessories	1	15	0
Leather Bound Canvas Case to carry Camera ready for exposure, an extra filmbox and accessories	2	0	0

J.A. Prestwich & Company's early premises in Lansdowne Road, Tottenham (c.1900).

J.A. Prestwich workshop in Lansdowne Road, Tottenham c.1900. Note that the stovepipe, in the foreground, has been removed to allow the photographer a better view.

It was not long before the growing success of the business required extra space and Prestwich was fortunate to acquire a disused chapel situated next to No.1, Lansdowne Road. By 1903, with a workforce of 50, it was now possible for Prestwich to produce motorcycle engines on a commercial scale from a design which he had begun sometime earlier. The 293cc J.A.P. engine was incorporated by the Triumph Cycle Company of Birmingham into one of their machines. At the time the motorcycle industry was going through an uncertain phase in the vehicle's popularity. However, the J.A.P. engine, which was made to exacting standards, was reported to be so reliable that its introduction was said to have founded the motorcycle industry in Britain. In fact J.A.P. made the proud claim that the "extreme accuracy", by which their components were manufactured, had been achieved by "grinding to limit gauges". The Company further claimed that at the time, the J.A.P. engine was "the first in the world to have its cylinder bores, pistons and piston rings, and all other hardened steel parts ground to gauges".

The J.A.P. "Dual Car" fitted with a 4.5hp engine, 1905.

Between 1903 and 1909 J.A.P. not only manufactured motorcycle engines but complete machines and even experimented with early motor car construction. It was a J.A.P. engine which powered the historic flight of A.V. Roe's triplane on 13th July 1909, when it became

An example of an early (1908) J.A.P. motorcycle. There were several earlier models.

the first all-British aircraft to fly with a British pilot. For a time Prestwich and Roe were in partnership, forming the J.A.P. Avroplane Company, but this enterprise was short lived.

The J.A.P. monoplane flying over Tottenham marshes in 1909.

Not long after Roe's flight, Prestwich saw his own monoplane built at his factory and fly from the Tottenham marshes, piloted by H.J. Harding, a local aeronautical enthusiast who had collaborated in the project. However, when flying over the Lea Valley, a local farmer complained that the noise from Harding's engine disturbed and unsettled his horses and Tottenham Council withdrew permission to use the marshes for take offs and landings. The ban by the local council appears to have been repeated by other authorities and, as a consequence, the aircraft was unable to fly anywhere in the country. To overcome the ban, Harding took the aircraft to France where he received a flying certificate and on returning to Britain he probably took great delight in flying the aircraft at the Blackpool Aero Show.

A Cooper light racing car powered by a J.A.P. 500cc engine c.1950.

Machinery in the J.A. Prestwich workshop in Lansdowne Road, Tottenham (c.1895).

A speedway racing bike c.1950 with a J.A.P. 500cc engine. The sport of speedway became very popular after the Second World War, with many teams competing in a league system. J.A.P. had a monopoly of this market.

As motorcycling gained popularity with the general public, demand for engines increased and J.A.P. received orders from leading motorcycle manufacturers Matchless, Royal Ruby and Royal Enfield. No doubt the pressure to produce more engines had been partially provoked by J.A.P. itself through a policy, which had been adopted some years earlier, of not competing directly with customers by producing complete motorcycles. It had also been decided to stop aircraft engine production and to concentrate the manufacturing effort on the popular motorcycle engine.

Production at Lansdowne Road had long outstripped the small workshop's capacity and in January 1911, manufacturing was transferred to a new plant in Northumberland Park, Tottenham, which had been designed for future expansion. The move was to prove timely as, during the lead up to the First World War (1914-18),

Picture showing approximately half of the capstan lathe bay of the J.A.P. Northumberland Park factory c.1950. At the time there were nineteen bays of machinery in operation.

the British government had begun to increase the level of contracts placed with the company. These were for various types of munitions, aircraft parts and motorcycle engines. As the war progressed and skilled men left the factory to become part of the conflict, women were employed to take on the production work.

At the cessation of hostilities, business for J.A.P. dramatically increased as former German customers returned and placed annual orders for 35,000 engines. In the post-war period, new racing engines were designed to keep J.A.P. in the forefront of motorcycle technology. Like many companies, J.A.P. suffered during the depression of the late 1920s and early 1930s but was saved by the tenacity of its owner and by adopting a flexible manufacturing policy.

A turning point in J.A.P.'s lagging fortune came in the years leading up to the Second World War, with the development of a portable, air-cooled, industrial petrol engine. The launch of this design could not have come at a better time for Britain or J.A.P. and with the introduction of a new water-cooled engine to take on heavier work the company was able to provide some 240,000 units in support of the war effort. These highly reliable engines performed numerous

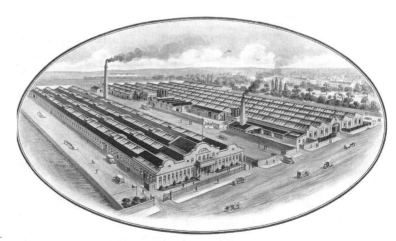

An artist's impression of J.A. Prestwich & Company's Northumberland Park factory, c.1915.

THE HOUSE THAT J.A.P. BUILT

1895   J. A. PRESTWICH & CO
TOTTENHAM, LONDON, N.   1915

tasks all over the world; powering tractors, pumping water, driving machinery and generating electricity. As in the First World War, J.A.P. manufactured munitions and other equipment on a huge scale for the allied forces, producing some ten million time and percussion fuses, twenty-three million small contact fuses and in excess of five and a quarter million aircraft parts. This was apart from engine and other production.

Although J.A.P. prospered directly after the war and made several innovative contributions to engine design, the firm – like many other Lea Valley companies in the early 1960s – was forced to succumb to increasing pressure, brought about in the main by overseas competition. The Northumberland Park factory finally closed its gates for good on 21st August 1963. However, there is no doubt that John Alfred Prestwich, through his pioneering work and dedication to excellence over many years, had helped perfect the mass production of a range of affordable, reliable and versatile engines which had a marked effect on the quality of life of many people throughout the world.

REFERENCES

Buchanan, D.J., *The J.A.P. Story, 1895-1951*, J.A. Prestwich, Tottenham, London, 1951.

Clew, Jeff, *J.A.P. - The Vintage Years*, Haynes Publishing Group, Yeovil, Somerset, 1985.

Clew, Jeff, *J.A.P. - The End of an Era*, Haynes Publishing Group, Yeovil, Somerset, 1988.

5. THE ART AND MYSTERY OF THE FLOATING SOLID

O n a cold March day in the early 1840s, with a keen east wind blowing along London's East India Road, a young George Corby Mackrow made his way from his home in Limehouse Fields to the works of Ditchburn and Mare. There, the lad was to discover whether he would like to learn the art and mystery of shipbuilding. The mystery being that he, as well as others of the day, expected a dry log of wood to always float when thrown into the water, but found it difficult to grasp the concept of how a ship made from iron did not sink.

An engraving showing part of the inside of the C.J. Mare & Company shipbuilding works at Blackwall, east London, c.1854. Note the giant Nasmyth steam hammer (named after the famous Victorian engineer, James Nasmyth) towards the centre of the picture. Mare's works had seven of these heavy stamping tools.

Previously, the young Mackrow had tried coopering, silversmithing and optical instrument making, none of which were to his liking. However, it would appear that Mackrow quickly found his vocation as a few weeks after his arrival he signed a seven-year apprenticeship agreement with the company. There is no doubt that the lad had chosen the right trade, as some years later he was

to rise to the office of chief naval architect to the company, making him responsible for all technical aspects of marine design and construction. This promotion would seem to indicate that Mackrow had indeed solved the puzzle of the floating solid.

An engraving showing a general view of the C.J. Mare & Company shipbuilding works at Blackwall in east London, c.1854. On the left bank of the waterway is the Essex yard and on the right bank the Middlesex yard. The waterway is the River Lea just before it enters the River Thames. This section of the Lea is known as Bow Creek.

The shipyard of Ditchburn and Mare was situated on the Middlesex bank of the River Lea, close to where the waterway enters the River Thames, an area commonly known as Leamouth. On maps, this section of the river is referred to as Bow Creek. By the mid 1840s the yard was finding it difficult to obtain supplies of iron at competitive rates. Bringing in the material by rail would have been expensive, as the main line ran through Stratford, some distance from the yard. If Stratford had been used, it would have meant transferring iron to horse-drawn wagons for the final part of the journey. At the time, the North Woolwich branch of the Eastern Counties and Thames Junction railway had not been completed.

To resolve the yard's difficulties Mare suggested to his partner that they should set up their own facility to roll iron plate. Clearly Ditchburn was not sympathetic to the idea and the partnership dissolved. In 1846, the new firm of C.J. Mare & Co. was established on the opposite side of the River Lea in Essex. The move was to mark a significant milestone in the history of British shipbuilding.

Looking through the eyes of Mackrow, the young apprentice, we

Bow Creek looking south
towards the River Thames as
it appeared in 1998.

learn that Mare was a particularly single-minded man who was prepared to face considerable odds to see his convictions through. It has been suggested that Mare's new venture had been considered decidedly foolhardy by many. One of Mackrow's early jobs was to mark, with wooden stakes, the site for two slips where ship and boatbuilding could commence. Apparently Mackrow and his fellow workmates nicknamed the site "Frog Island" and we are told that the rushes which grew there on the swampy ground came up to his waist. During the period of the spring tides much of the site became submerged. Nevertheless, Mare was initially successful in laying down eight boats for the Citizen Company, which was one of two sizeable operators plying their trade on the Thames.

The coming of the Crimean War in 1853 saw an increase in both wood and iron shipbuilding. Mare's yard received orders not only from the British Admiralty but also from the French government. It is recorded that the yard built four wooden despatch vessels, four gunboats, two large despatch boats and some twelve iron mortar boats. Two floating batteries were also constructed for the French government, comprising a wooden shell plated with 3.5 inches (9cm) of armour. These were to be used for attacking the fortified coastal positions at the Crimea.

By 1856 Mare was in financial difficulty and the running of the company was taken over by his father-in-law, Peter Rolt, who assumed control as chairman. The company name was changed to the Thames Ironworks & Shipbuilding Co. Soon, the new company was bidding for a British Admiralty contract to construct what was to become the largest warship afloat, the first seagoing ironclad in

A bank of four restored washing machines in the laundry area on board *H.M.S. Warrior*. Note the handle, currently reversed to prevent accidents, which was used to revolve the clothes in the tubs. Also note that each machine has its own mangle to squeeze water from the clothes after washing.

H.M.S. Warrior's restored wardroom where the officers would dine. In time of battle the dining table would become the operating table.

View, looking along part of the upper deck towards the stern, of the restored *H.M.S. Warrior*.

the world. *H.M.S. Warrior*, powered by both sail and steam, was launched in December 1860 and was accepted into service by the Royal Navy. Despite being clad with 4 inches (10cm) of iron plate and weighing 9,210 tons, *H.M.S. Warrior* could achieve 17.5 knots with both power sources engaged.

It is difficult today to imagine that large-scale manufacturing industries such as ironworks and shipbuilding were operating at the southern end of the River Lea. Normally such industries are associated with Scotland, Northern Ireland and north east England. Between the years 1840 and 1911 the Thames Ironworks, including sixteen years of C.J. Mare, was responsible for the construction of 278 merchant ships.

H.M.S. Warrior, launched 29th December 1860, was, at the time, the largest sea-going iron-clad warship in the world.

H.M.S. Thunderer (22,500 tons, Dreadnought Class), the last major warship built at the Thames Ironworks, was launched on 1st February 1911.

A breech-loading Armstrong 110-pounder gun mounted to the fore of the restored *H.M.S. Warrior.* Note the brass slide and pivot tracks fastened to the deck which were used for positioning the gun.

Perhaps even more remarkably, the Thames Ironworks, including ten years of C.J. Mare, built 144 warships. The last to be built at the yard was the 22,500-ton battleship *Thunderer*, which saw service with the Royal Navy during the First World War at the Battle of Jutland.

The Thames Ironworks, in its heyday, ran six departments. These were: marine engines and motorcars, boatbuilding, cranes, electrical engineering, civil engineering and shipbuilding. During the company's remarkable history it was involved in producing ironwork for a number of diverse civil engineering projects. These

The Britannia Bridge over the Menai Straits under construction in c.1849 with box girders supplied by C.J. Mare & Company.

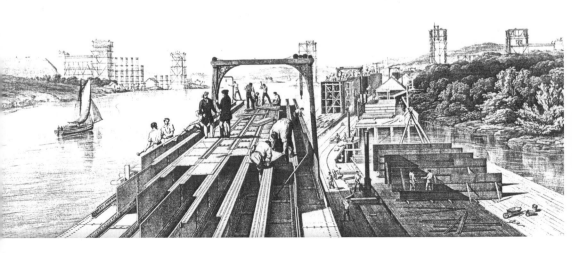

I.K. Brunel's Royal Albert Bridge which took the railway over the River Tamar to Saltash in Cornwall. Built in 1859, and still in operation today (2009), with girders supplied by the Thames Ironworks.

included the roof of Alexandra Palace, fabricated sections for Westminster Bridge, Hammersmith Bridge and the Menai Bridge and the construction of gates for Barry Docks in Wales.

Perhaps one of the most spectacular high-profile civil engineering projects, for which the Thames Ironworks acted as a supplier, was Isambard Kingdom Brunel's Royal Albert Bridge (1848–59) which took the railway over the River Tamar to Saltash in Cornwall. Here 2,650 tons of wrought iron and 1,200 tons of cast iron were used. Some of the individual spans weighed in the order of 1,060 tons.

It is therefore quite probable, particularly with the earlier Brunel connection, that the Thames Ironworks could have supplied iron to build the Great Eastern. For a ship of the day it was an enormous size, weighing 18,915 tons and being constructed from 30,000 separate iron plates, each held with 100 rivets. At her launch, in 1858, she was the largest ship afloat, having been designed to carry enough fuel to circumnavigate the globe without stopping. The Great Eastern was built at John Scott Russell's Millwall yard which was only about a mile distant from the Thames Ironworks. This would have made it a simple task for Brunel to discuss his material requirements with the Leamouth yard.

In the latter part of the nineteenth and early twentieth century, the Thames Ironworks Shipbuilding & Engineering Co., as it had become known, suffered from a diminishing number of orders from the British Admiralty. Arnold Hills, who had joined the board in 1880, was convinced that the company was experiencing unfair treatment from the Admiralty and he was also of the view that the northern shipyards were operating a price ring. In 1911 Hill petitioned Winston Churchill, then First Lord of the Admiralty, but received little sympathy. December 1912 saw the closure of the Thames Ironworks with the loss of over seventy years know-how. When viewing the episode from the twenty-first century, it does seem curious that government ministers would allow this to happen. With clear indicators of the coming conflict in Europe (the First World War was less than two years away) one would have expected the British government to have found ways of supporting this talented company with its highly skilled workforce.

Today, in West Ham United Football Club, the memory of the Thames Ironworks lives on. The club's emblem of crossed hammers is a graphic reminder of its Thames Ironworks founding origins.

REFERENCES

Banbury, Philip, *Shipbuilders of the Thames and Medway*, David and Charles, Newton Abbot, 1971.

Falconer, John, *What's Left of Brunel*, Dial House, Surrey, 1995.

Larken, Meriel, *1862: Vapor Yavari, Navigation on Lake Titicaca*, Peru, Asociacion Peruano Britanica, 2006.

Mackrow, G.C., "Some Reminiscences of the Early Days of the Thames Iron Works and Shipbuilding Company", *Thames Iron Works Gazette*, Vol.1, 1895.

Mackrow, G.C., "Some Reminiscences of the Early Days of the Thames Iron Works and Shipbuilding Company", *Thames Iron Works Gazette*, Vol.2, 1896.

Powell, W.R. (ed.), *West Ham 1886-1986,* Council of the London Borough of Newham, London, 1986.

6. A TINY SEED IS PLANTED AND A NOISY FLOWER BLOSSOMS IN THE LEA VALLEY

Household names in the car industry call on Lotus as engineering consultants and problem solvers. The Lea Valley, over the years, has been home to and a source of many accounts of invention, entrepreneurship and inspiration. The story of Lotus is certainly no exception.

Anthony Colin Bruce Chapman, acknowledged by his peers as "one of the greatest racing car designers and engineers of all time", was born on the 19th May 1928 in Richmond, Surrey. At the time of his birth his father was the proprietor of a local public house, the Orange Tree. A little before the start of the Second World War the family moved to north London and took over the running of the Railway Hotel in Tottenham Lane, Hornsey. Colin, as he had become more familiarly known, was sent to the nearby Stationers' Company School.

Anthony Colin Bruce Chapman (1928–82), founder of Lotus.

From an early school report, when Colin was ten, we are given a privileged glimpse of the young lad's emerging talent and temperament. The report shows that Colin came top of his class and received a merit award for his efforts, achieving outstanding percentage marks of 98 and 85 respectively for arithmetic and drawing. His form master, when assessing Colin's performance, gives us a clue to the way the boy's character was developing, when he wrote, "He is very willing and helpful and shows considerable efficiency in his work. His impulsiveness leads to far too many detentions". These had amounted to eleven in the past academic year alone. From these early observations of talent and individualism, it might be fair to conclude that we could predict the emergence of an engineering intellect that would eventually mature into a mind of pure inventive genius.

After wartime evacuation to the comparative safety of Wisbech in Cambridgeshire, Colin returned to London and entered University College in October 1945 to study engineering. Although he reportedly had a quick and absorbing mind, it would appear that he was not the ideal student. At the time he seemed more interested in a Muswell Hill girl, Hazel Williams (his future wife), motorcycles and, what was to become his lifetime passion, cars. However, despite these distractions, he graduated in 1948 as a civil engineer, having specialised in structural engineering. During his time at college he had joined the University Air Squadron where he learned to fly and, according to his biographer, Jabby Crombac, the experience was to have a profound influence upon Chapman's approach to solving engineering design problems. Through flying he had learned the

Colin Chapman's early advertisements for business, some inviting potential customers to "call and discuss your problems with us".

basics of aerodynamics, a science that would help him when designing cars in the future.

While at college, Colin Chapman's quick brain had allowed him to assimilate information easily and this had given him time away from studies to indulge his entrepreneurial skills. Pooling resources with a fellow student, Colin Dare, the pair took advantage of a post-war opportunity by exploiting the scarcity of new cars in the marketplace through buying up old vehicles of dubious quality, repairing them and selling them on for a quick profit. Before long the business had grown and the two students were reported to be selling one car a week.

There is always pressure in an embryonic venture of this sort to turn stock around quickly if a healthy cash flow is to be maintained; otherwise the business becomes vulnerable to unexpected market changes. Unfortunately, the business of the two students suffered two damaging blows, one internal and the other external. First Colin Dare failed his first year exams and dropped out of college, leaving his partner to carry on alone. This Colin Chapman did until beset with blow number two when, in late 1947, the government withdrew the basic petrol ration, a wartime economy measure. With the availability of more petrol, consumer demand for new cars increased and the established vehicle manufacturers responded to the challenge. This effectively put an end to the rapid car sales and the remaining stock – which had been deliberately built up during the profitable times – was sold off at a loss. However, one ancient 1930 Austin Seven saloon could not be sold so Colin, while still at college, decided to turn the vehicle into a "special". In a lock-up garage, rented from Hazel's father, he worked on the car for almost a year, replacing the original body with one made from marine plywood which he covered with aluminium to give the chassis added rigidity. In 1948 the completed car was registered for road use with a number OX 9292. Rather than keep the name Austin, Colin decided to give the car a different image befitting the new shape. He called it the Lotus Mk I. It is not really known why this name was chosen and according to Colin Chapman's biographer he never revealed the secret. Colin and Hazel took the car around the country, entering it in a number of hill climbs and trials and it is reported that they had a reasonable degree of success in these events.

After graduation in 1948, Colin had already gained his Private Pilot's Licence through the University Air Squadron; he accepted a short-term commission with the Royal Air Force, as he had to complete his compulsory National Service. His biographer believes that

Hazel Williams (later Mrs Chapman) at the wheel of the very first Lotus Mk I. Note the partially completed body, which had flat alloy-bonded plywood panels to improve the car's rigidity.

accepting the commission was mainly for the purpose of "getting in plenty of flying at someone else's expense". During periods of leave from the RAF, Colin began work on what was to become his Lotus Mk II; this was a more adventurous project than his first car. Although still based on the Austin Seven, the vehicle now had independent front suspension, made from modified Ford components. In June 1950 the car was entered in a five-lap race at Silverstone, with Colin as the driver. This was Colin's first motor race, which he won, beating a Bugatti into second place. No doubt encouraged by this initial success, Colin went on to gain a further twenty-one awards in the Mk II before the season finished.

One day in late 1950, when driving with Hazel, along Vallance Road, Wood Green, north London, Colin noticed a number of cars that were being worked on in the garden of a large Edwardian house. He stopped and introduced himself to the two young men, Michael and Nigel Allen, who were working on the vehicles, and asked whether they would like to join him in building racing cars. The brothers readily agreed and later Colin introduced them to another contact, Rodney Nuckey, who had a tool and die company (Nuckey Scott-Brown Co.) not far away in Alexandra Park Road. Here, Colin was already working on his Lotus Mk III with Rodney. Again this was based on an Austin Seven. Now, with the addition of the brothers' engineering skill and in particular the use of their equipment, which he did not possess, Colin was able to incorporate his innovative ideas into his new model. The 1951 racing season saw the car entered for some thirty-two events, when remarkably it gained fourteen first and thirteen second places.

Teaming up with the Allen brothers was yet another of Colin

Chapman's great ideas for advancing his passion to build racing cars. This he could now achieve without having to incur the high capital costs which were usually encountered during the initial stages of a manufacturing company start-up. The brothers had established a well-equipped workshop with oxy-acetylene welding equipment, metal cutters, lifting gear, a drill press, lathe and inspection pit, alongside their parents' house, so it is easy to see why they had been chosen. However, building and testing racing cars, often into the early hours of the morning, is not the best way to get on with your neighbours in a leafy London suburb. Not unnaturally the situation came to a head when the residents brought a petition before the local authority after first withholding their property rates as a protest against their lack of peace and quiet. Fortunately, there was a solution to the problem, as not far away, behind the Railway Hotel in Tottenham Lane, there were some old stables and a bottle store owned by Colin's father, Stan. Colin was able to persuade his father to let him rent the buildings and convert them into workshop space. In January 1952, after much alteration by Colin and a band of volunteers, which included Hazel, the premises were ready for the move from Vallance Road.

The success of the Mk III had brought many enquiries, particularly from competitors in the race business, for technical assistance, parts and modifications. Therefore, on 1st January 1952 the decision was taken to register officially the Lotus Engineering Company with Colin Chapman and Michael Allen as shareholders. Nigel Allen did not join his brother in the new venture, but instead decided to return to his earlier studies and follow the profession of his father as a dentist. However, he did help as much as he could during his spare time.

After Colin was demobilised from the RAF he had begun a job with the British Aluminium Company (BAC) in their west London office in St James's Street. When he formed Lotus Engineering with Michael he was still employed full time by BAC. It had been decided that until the new business became financially viable Colin would continue with his day job, to bring in a little cash, and work at Lotus during evenings and at weekends. Michael would work for Lotus full time, while Hazel would work during her spare time, packing customers' orders and typing letters. At the time, orders were received for complete trials cars and there was also a growing demand for Lotus's innovative designs and engineering expertise. Soon the business was beginning to creak at the seams and there were delays in fulfilling customer orders. The lack of full-time staff was clearly a major problem and it would appear that the business only just kept going by relying on a number of skilled sub-contractors.

On the advice of Colin's father and, with £25 borrowed from Hazel, it was decided that the time had come to reform the business from a partnership into a limited liability company. On 25th September 1952 the new business was registered (number 511696) and renamed the Lotus Engineering Company Limited. Shortly afterwards Michael Allen resigned, due to the pressure of work which had caused him to put in long hours to try and keep the business afloat. It would also seem that, like many other business relationships, disagreements had begun to occur between the founders as to how the company should be run. Now with relationships strained and the daily task of hand to mouth operation, Lotus was teetering on the edge of financial collapse.

By January 1953 Colin Chapman and his girlfriend Hazel Williams were in control of the business and Colin had effectively become an evening director. Colin's father, Stan, who appears in the early days to have had a fair measure of control over his son, would not allow him to leave his day job at BAC and concentrate his energies full time on running the business. This did not occur until the end of 1954, after marriage to Hazel on 16th October of that year. Somehow Hazel still managed to cope with her component packing duties plus the general day-to-day administration, while at the same time working at her mother's haberdashery shop in Muswell Hill, north London. With the structural changes in place and Colin's untiring determination to succeed, the business was about to alter direction yet again. With money again borrowed from Hazel, Colin ordered six Mark VI space frame chassis from a former school friend, John Teycenne, who, with partner David Kelsey, had recently started a welding business called the Progress Chassis Company. This was in a shed at the back of his parents' home in Ribbledale Road, Hornsey, a few hundred yards from the Railway Hotel (later the company would move to First Avenue, Edmonton north London). The chassis ordered was a fully stressed multi-tubular design of Colin's, consisting of both round and square sections. In the previous year he had poured much of his structural engineering talent into the design of this unique product. Now, based on the new chassis, Colin's big idea was to sell component kits of race-proven cars. The kits would not attract the very prohibitive government purchase tax which, at the time, was levied on all new vehicles and accounted for around two-thirds of a car's purchase price. However, to take the project forward Colin would need to build at least one "works demonstrator" and this would require people, a luxury he could not afford. This was yet another problem for Colin Chapman to solve and he did this through an amazing network of acquaintances and connections within the engineering industry. A number of these contacts were enthusiasts who built and raced Austin Seven "specials". Many of them were associated with the 750 Motor Club, of which Colin was a member. The trick now was to get skilled volunteers to work unpaid for the reformed Lotus Company. Fortunately, it would appear that the chance to become involved at Lotus presented a wonderful opportunity for a number of enthusiastic builders and would-be racing drivers who wished to indulge their hobby and to have fun.

By the middle of 1953, with four Lotus Mk VIs successfully competing, the car was becoming noticed by the international press. The publicity brought interest from abroad and by the end of the year orders for twenty cars had been received. At about this time, with the car involved in regular outings at race meetings, it was decided that a team name was needed and Team Lotus Limited was born. Colin Chapman's big idea was paying off and after only a year of operation, Lotus finances were showing a profit.

Not content with the success of the Mk VI Colin wanted to push the bounds of motorcar engineering to the limit. Through one of Colin's volunteer workers, Mike Costin, who later became the "Cos" in the now famous Cosworth Engineering Company, he was introduced to Mike's brother, Frank. At the time Frank worked for the de Havilland Aircraft Company and was experienced in the science of aerodynamics. After much discussion, a drawing of a revolutionary shape was produced and Colin paid David Kelsey, of the Progress Chassis Company, to make a scale model. This was tested by Frank in a wind tunnel and returned to Colin with a number of suggested improvements. A local panel-beating company, Williams & Pritchard, were employed to produce the new body shape and the Progress Chassis Co. took on the work of building a re-designed chassis. When the new streamlined Lotus, now the Mk VIII, was entered for the British Grand Prix at Silverstone in July 1954 with Colin as the driver, it comfortably won the event, beating a "works" Porsche driven by Hans Herrmann into second place.

The future of Lotus was now looking secure and with growing orders for kits and new innovative designs the company could begin to take on permanent staff. With all the new business and the addition of the Mk IX and Mk X to the range, the need for more workshop space at Tottenham Lane became desperate. In 1956, with the backing of Stan Chapman and Fred Bushell, the company accountant, a piece of land was acquired next to the existing buildings. Money was raised and a two-storey extension built, which increased the workshop capacity by about a third, freeing up space for the production of Colin's next project. This was to be the Lotus Eleven and not a continuation of the "Mark" system. It also signalled the start of model names beginning with the letter "E". The development of the Eleven has been recognised as one of Colin Chapman's finest designs, incorporating all his best ideas. This car had a new chassis, engine, body and brakes but more importantly it was probably the first design in which a great deal of attention had been paid to allowing easy access to mechanical parts. The car proved to be a resounding success with famous names like Mike Hawthorn, Graham Hill, Innes Ireland, David Piper, Roy Salvadori and Alan Stacey acquiring them.

Colin Chapman's Hornsey showroom with a Lotus Elite on display. Within a few months of opening, the showroom was converted into an office.

With orders pouring in and the need to continue experimenting with novel materials, such as the moulded fibreglass body for the new Lotus Elite, company resources were being stretched to the limit. For a go-ahead company like Lotus there was always the necessity of having to monitor, modify and re-design critical components that had been subjected to high levels of stress during their exposure to motor racing. It seems, probably due to the pressure of work, that many of these tasks were carried out without too much scientific analysis, instead being replaced on a "suck it and see" basis. However, these tasks were becoming more frequent, particularly as Team Lotus was now very much part of the international Grand Prix scene, competing with established names like Ferrari and Maserati. The pressure that these duties put on the dozen or so staff at the Tottenham Lane works must have been enormous. If there were to be criticism of Colin Chapman it would be that he took on too much work. Also it is likely that he expected his staff to keep up the same deadly pace of long hours with few breaks that he himself endured. Having said that, without Colin burning the midnight oil for many years the company would not have progressed to its present position.

The Lotus showroom now being used (2000) by a well-known builders' merchant.

By 1958 it had become obvious that the Tottenham Lane site was inadequate for what was now an international business. After viewing and rejecting a number of local premises, a green-field site was finally purchased at Delamare Road, Cheshunt in the northern part of the Lea Valley. A mortgage was eventually secured and the building of two factory units commenced. One unit was allocated to Lotus Cars Ltd. (formerly Lotus Engineering Ltd.) and the other was shared by the racing arm, Team Lotus, and the newly formed Lotus Components Ltd. The move from Hornsey to Cheshunt took place in June 1959 although it was not until September of that year that production got fully underway. Lotus was to remain at Cheshunt for only six years and during this time the company increased in international stature as Colin Chapman's designs became more and more adventurous. World-famous drivers such as Stirling Moss drove his cars and he was collaborating with major manufacturers on aspects of racing car design. Although there were difficulties at Cheshunt, with delays to the Lotus–Cortina contract, Colin was now beginning to handle his project load more comfortably than before. This can be attributed to the dedicated staff he had managed to gather around him, who were recognised for having some of the best designing capabilities and engineering skills in the industry. The fact that he was able to attract and keep them is a tribute to Colin Chapman's considerable foresight and ability to enthuse.

In 1962 there were mounting difficulties with the supplier of bodies for the Lotus Elan over cost, quality and delivery. This provoked a swift decision to take the work in house. An empty factory was taken over in Delamare Road and within three months new bodies were being moulded and painted. However, it was decided to erect a new purpose-built plant on adjacent land owned by the company and as a consequence the necessary planning permission was sought. Although permission was eventually granted and a new body shop built, the facility was never used. Lotus had been somehow informed that they would not be allowed to further increase the number of buildings on the Cheshunt site. This was probably because the factory backed onto a housing estate and the neighbours were no doubt fed up with the noise of high performance engines revving up close to their back gardens. In an odd way this was a case of history repeating itself. A similar situation had occurred some ten years earlier (although on a much smaller scale) when complaints of noise and disturbance were reported by the neighbours of the Allen brothers, to the Local Authority, over their operating a car repair business in the front garden of their parents' home in Wood Green.

An aerial view of the Lotus site at Hethel, Norfolk.

The refusal to allow expansion of the Cheshunt facility forced Colin Chapman to look for a more suitable site where neighbourhood annoyance could be kept to a minimum and vehicle testing could take place without resorting to the use of local roads. With these criteria it would be difficult to find another site within the Lea Valley and the region was about to lose what had become a highly prestigious company. Towards the end of 1965, a former wartime airfield was purchased at Hethel in Norfolk, after negotiations with

The Lotus assembly line at Hethel, Norfolk.

A Lotus Elise under test in an anechoic chamber.

local farmers and the Norwich planning authority. Contractors were engaged and building of the new factory began in 1966. The move to Norfolk took place across one weekend in November of that year with half of the 500 workforce electing for transfer. Production of vehicles stopped at Cheshunt on the Friday night and at 4pm on Monday afternoon the first Hethel-produced car was ready.

In this short space, we have summarised the development of one man's hobby into a multi-million pound business, which is now the technical envy of the world. In America, a new testing facility and engineering centre has been set up that will be an extension of Lotus Engineering's UK high-tech operations. This was achieved

An image of a Lotus concept ice vehicle.

A Lotus-designed five-wheel shopping trolley.

when the Michigan Automotive Research Corporation (MARCO) was acquired in April 2000 and is a further example of the determination of Lotus to stay ahead of the field.

With pressures from consumers and governments upon motor manufacturers worldwide to reduce CO_2 emissions dramatically and to come up with greener technologies, Lotus Engineering, the automotive consultancy division of Lotus, has been developing new ways to synthesise external sound on electric and hybrid vehicles. This is to help alleviate consumer concern that "quiet" vehicles could pose a serious threat of injury to both pedestrians and cyclists. To warn the public of an approaching vehicle with this

The Lotus-designed Olympic bicycle.

The stunning Lotus Evora.

hybrid technology, a demonstrator car has been built which simulates engine sound when the vehicle is in motion. This is just one of many innovative ideas and solutions coming from the Lotus team of talented engineers that keeps the company at the forefront of technological development.

Colin Chapman would have been justly proud of the progress made by his company from its humble beginning in Hornsey north London to a major player on the world technology stage. Sadly he was unable to experience all the fruits of his early labours, as on 15th December 1982 he died prematurely from a heart attack at the age of fifty-four. A plaque has now been erected in his memory on the site where it all started at 7, Tottenham Lane, Hornsey in London's Lea Valley.

REFERENCES

Author unknown, "Lotus Engineering Expands into US", *Engineering Technology*, May 2000.

Author unknown, "The Lotus 50th Party", Lotus Cars Ltd., 12th September 1998.

Capel, Graham, *Lotus - Historic Half Century*, Historic Lotus Publications, 1998.

Crombac, Gerard, *Colin Chapman - The Man and his Cars*, Patrick Stephens Ltd., 1986.

Haskell, Hugh, *Colin Chapman Lotus Engineering - Theories, Designs and Applications*, Osprey Publishing, 1993.

Private conversations with Clive Chapman (Junior) and Graham Capel, June 2000. Graham Capel most generously sent the author an early draft of his forthcoming book, *The Early Years of Lotus*, as background information for this chapter.

Walters, Joanna, "Carmaker Barking for Rover", *Observer*, 27th August 2000.

Note 1
In 1986, 80 per cent of Lotus was sold to Proton, a Malaysian company, for £64 million.

Note 2
For a fuller treatment of the technical aspects of Lotus cars and their racing achievements, the reader is invited to refer to the references for this chapter.

Note 3
The Lotus flower has a long and interesting history and can be seen in hieroglyphics cut into the walls of many Egyptian tombs that date from 3,000 BC. It is also the symbol for the ancient region of Upper Egypt.

7. GEOFFREY DE HAVILLAND – MORE THAN A FLIGHT OF FANCY

Not all the Lea Valley companies that were eventually to become famous for inventing or designing world-beating products began their lives in the area and this was certainly true of de Havilland and its talented founder, although, at the start of his career there was a connection with the region.

Geoffrey de Havilland, the second son of Charles, the curate of Hazlemere, Buckinghamshire was born on 27th July 1882. Shortly afterwards his father took the parish of Nuneaton, Warwickshire and this is where Geoffrey, with his brothers Ivon and Hereward plus his sisters Ione and Gladys spent their early years. When Geoffrey was fourteen the family moved to a parish at Crux Easton, Hampshire and it was here that the young man first showed an early interest in things mechanical and scientific, when he and his brother Ivon installed a series of generators in the rectory to provide electricity.

Captain Sir Geoffrey de Havilland (1882–1965). This picture was taken in 1954.

After leaving Edward's School, Oxford at the age of seventeen the family expected Geoffrey to follow in his father's footsteps and enter the church. However, his interest in mechanics proved too strong and in 1900 he joined the Crystal Palace Engineering School where he received a solid grounding in the subject. After the engineering school Geoffrey appears to have become somewhat restless and his career was anything but settled. In 1903 he joined Williams & Robinson of Rugby as an apprentice, but by 1905 he had taken a job as draughtsman at the Wolseley Tool & Motor Car Company in Birmingham, leaving their employ after only one year. Geoffrey's next job brought him to London's Lea Valley where he took up a position in the design department of the embryonic Motor Omnibus Construction

Company then based in Hookers Lane, Walthamstow. The company, founded in January 1905 by Arthur Salisbury-Jones a member of the Stock Exchange, was to become, in 1912, the Associated Equipment Company Limited (AEC), the forerunner of London Transport, now called Transport for London.

While working for the Motor Omnibus Construction Company Geoffrey became friendly with Frank Hearle, a young mechanic who worked at the Dalston bus garage in east London. No doubt sharing the same interests gave the young men the idea of pooling their skills and working together and in 1907 they rented a flat in Kensington, west London. Somehow, Geoffrey persuaded his sister Ione to join them to carry out the domestic chores. It must have been a reasonably amicable arrangement as later Frank proposed and Ione became Mrs Hearle.

On 17th December 1903, the Wright brothers, Wilbur and Orville were the first to make a sustained and controlled powered flight in a heavier than air machine. On that historic day, from the sands at Kitty Hawk in North Carolina, USA, the brothers made four flights. The longest of these lasted fifty-nine seconds and covered a distance of 852 feet (260m). In August 1908, Wilbur Wright took his aircraft to Europe and began giving demonstrations in France and it was this that gave Geoffrey de Havilland the inspiration for his new career as he now saw his future in flight. With £1,000 borrowed from his grandfather and the help of his friend Frank Hearle, he set about designing and constructing his first aircraft. In May 1909, he took time out to marry a family friend Louie Thomas. Louie had formally been employed as a governess to Geoffrey's younger brothers and sisters. It was not long before Geoffrey had his new wife helping with the construction of his aeroplane.

Geoffrey's first aircraft was not a success but he persevered and in early 1910 he was able to fly his second machine. As his piloting skills grew and he became more confident he took Frank Hearle for a flight. A little later his wife Louie, and their eight-week-old son Geoffrey Raoul, were also transported aloft. For an early aviation pioneer this would seem to be a rather foolhardy act to have carried out, or it just might be that Geoffrey de Havilland was supremely self assured in his growing piloting skills and also highly confident in the design of his second aircraft.

In 1911, obviously impressed with the design of de Havilland's aircraft, the Army's Balloon Factory at Farnborough, Hampshire bought the machine and Geoffrey was taken on as a pilot and aircraft designer - quite an achievement for someone who had taught himself to fly. One year later, the Army's factory became the Royal Aircraft Factory and de Havilland then took the opportunity to join the Special Reserve of the Royal Flying Corps. De Havilland's flying career was progressing at a pace and then, in 1913, tragedy struck when he was involved in a serious crash. By 1914, probably because of the injuries he had sustained, the Royal Aircraft Factory changed his job to that of Inspector of Aeroplanes. For a man with de Havilland's drive and ambition this was not the career path that he wanted so he resigned his position and went to work for the Aircraft Manufacturing Company (Airco).

On 4th August 1914 Britain declared war on Germany and entered the growing conflict of the Great War. As a reservist, de Havilland received his call-up papers and was drafted into the Royal Flying Corps. Due to his previous injuries he was prevented from active service on the Western Front and was confined to patrolling the sea off the east coast and also the seas off Scotland. The war created considerable pressures for the aircraft industry, which already lacked talented aircraft designers and de Havilland was soon recalled to Airco to continue his work. Here he produced a number of successful designs that were put into production, and for which he received a royalty for each aircraft built.

When the conflict ended in 1918 de Havilland had become quite wealthy, allowing him the luxury of buying a large house in Edgware. In October that year a third son John was born, his second son Peter Jason having been born in 1913. Just when everything seemed to be going so well for him, with the end of the war and the enlargement of his family, de Havilland suffered a nervous breakdown, thought to have been brought about by pressure of work during the war years. To help relieve him of pressure the family moved to Balcombe in Sussex as this was considered to be a more peaceful location. However, the move seems to have heightened rather lessened de Havilland's anxieties as he was now too far away from his work. The family took the decision to move once again, this time to Stanmore, Middlesex.

The frantic developments in manufacturing during the Great War had seen the production of military aircraft go from 53 machines a month during the early period to 2,669 a month by the end. When peacetime came the industry was brought to a virtual standstill almost overnight, as there was now a surplus of military aircraft. Factories that had traditionally manufactured other products before the war and had been either taken over by the government or drawn into the war effort as contractors, supplying parts and material, reverted back to their established trades. However, some manufacturers, because of loss of orders, went into liquidation. After such dramatic changes within the British aircraft industry it was clear that restructuring would have to take place and those remaining manufacturers would need to concentrate their efforts on the commercial market rather than the military.

As a result of the changing requirements of Britain's aircraft industry in the post-war years, and no doubt in an endeavour to consolidate their manufacturing base, the Birmingham Small Arms Company (BSA) took over Airco, Geoffrey de Havilland's former place of work.

As often happens, the loss of a job creates new opportunities and Geoffrey took a life-changing decision. With £3,000 of his own money together with another £1,000 raised, probably from colleagues and acquaintances, and the backing of his former Airco employer George Holt Thomas, who put £10,000 into the new enterprise, on 25th September 1920 Geoffrey founded the de Havilland Aircraft Company. A lease was taken out on the site of the former London & Provincial Flying School at Stag Lane, Edgware. Frank Hearle, his friend from the days of the Motor Omnibus Construction Company, was appointed works manager, and de Havilland assumed responsibility for aircraft design.

The first task of the new company was to complete two unfinished DH.18 biplane aircraft that had been started by Airco before they were taken over by BSA. These aircraft were modified with improved engine mountings and undercarriages and became the DH.18A. The aircraft were then sold to embryonic commercial airlines and operated on the Croydon–Paris and other continental routes. Geoffrey de Havilland saw that the future lay in designing and building new commercial aircraft rather than in the risky military market and this was the direction in which he would take his company.

While some today might believe that the developing commercial airline market of the 1920s would be a wise area in which to invest, in reality it carried considerable financial risks. As might be imagined with an early airline start-up industry the technology, particularly that related to electronic communication and navigation, had yet to develop as a medium that aircrew and ground staff could rely upon. International safety rules for airlines had a long way to go and passengers had yet to be convinced that flying, rather than travelling by ship or train was the safest and cheapest option. In April 1922 early public confidence in flying had been dealt a severe blow when the world's first mid-air collision occurred over France, killing seven people. Reports of other aircraft crashes on take off and landing had also dented people's faith in the new way to travel. The culmination of these tragic events had caused some of the early airlines to go into liquidation and this was bad news for any embryonic aircraft manufacturer who was looking to secure fresh orders.

Anyone starting up in business requires a degree of luck and this came to Geoffrey de Havilland in the shape of the wealthy businessman Alan Samuel Butler who approached him to order a new aeroplane. Butler must have noticed something special about Geoffrey de Havilland's set up as he invested heavily in the company and, as a further mark of his growing confidence in the business, he became chairman in 1924. Over the next ten years the Stag Lane factory produced a number of highly successful aircraft designs, one of the most famous being the Gipsy Moth (DH.60). This aircraft won the King's Cup Air Race in 1928 and the publicity the machine received from this and its many other aerial achievements gave it an international reputation and also a worldwide market. By the end of 1929 the Stag Lane factory was turning out three machines per day, a remarkable achievement for the pioneering industry. The DH.60 was even manufactured in America and also in France. In 1931 the Air Ministry requested a re-designed DH.60 as a training aircraft for the Royal Air Force and the model became the now famous Tiger Moth (DH.82).

De Havilland DH.84 Dragon at Stag Lane, 1932.

A rather bent de Havilland DH.9J (G-EBEZ) at the Stag Lane de Havilland School of Flying, 1930.

By 1932 the strong demand for aircraft and the expansion of London's suburban housing around the Stag Lane factory made it difficult for de Havilland to continue at the Edgware site. Fortunately de Havilland had seen the problems coming and had purchased land in 1930 to build a new factory at Hatfield, Hertfordshire. As a further precaution, to reduce the risk of future housing encroachment, farmland was acquired adjacent to the new site. The Stag Lane airfield was closed in 1934 but the factory was retained for the production of aero engines.

De Havilland DH.88 Comet E–1 in flight at Hatfield Aerodrome, 1934.

As the decade progressed, airlines began to request larger machines, as confidence grew in the safety and reliability of aircraft designed by companies such as de Havilland. This new phase in the development of more complex aircraft meant that large teams of designers were now engaged in the work. Geoffrey, realistically but probably reluctantly, had now to take a back seat, not just in designing but also his test-flying activities, curtailed by the complexities of the latest larger aircraft. The first of the series of multi-engined biplanes began with the twin-engine Dragon. This aircraft became popular with airlines across the world. Airlines like Imperial Airways and Qantas took the four-engined Express Air Liner (DH.86) for routes over long stretches of water. A two-engined cut-down version of the DH.86, the Dragon Rapide (known later as just Rapide), became one of the world's most successful aircraft used by airlines.

An inside view of the hangers at Hatfield under construction, with what appears to be a Gypsy Moth aircraft in the middle foreground.

An aerial view of Hatfield Aerodrome, 1930.

A craftsman operating a lathe in the de Havilland propeller and engine shop at Stag Lane, Edgware, c.1940.

Arthur Hagg, the Chief Designer at Hatfield and his team had been experimenting with new technologies in wooden aircraft construction and had produced a strong, light material that, except in torsion, could match weight for weight the strength of duralumin or steel in flight. The team had produced a new material by gluing together a sandwich of balsa between two layers of plywood and from this an aircraft fuselage and wings could be constructed. These construction techniques were first tried out on the twin-engined Comet Racer, which won the London to Australia race in 1934. The first large aircraft to incorporate the new material, designed to an Air Ministry specification, was the Albatross (DH.91), a beautiful looking four-engined plane that was used as an experimental high-speed transatlantic mail-plane in 1939.

Imperial Airways de Havilland Albatross (G-AEVV) being refuelled at Hatfield Aerodrome, 1938.

When the Second World War began, the de Havilland Company was producing the popular Rapides, Tiger Moths and Airspeed Oxfords for the Royal Air Force. After commencement of hostilities, other aircraft from the factory were acquired by the Air Ministry and used for training or transport. In 1940, de Havilland bought the shares of the Airspeed Company and the design offices were merged with his own and later moved to Salisbury Hall near St Albans, Hertfordshire. Alfred Hessell Tiltman and Nevil Shute Norway (the latter was not just an aeronautical engineer but also the famous author Nevil Shute) had founded the Airspeed Company in York in 1931. In 1934 the firm was taken over by the shipbuilder Swan Hunter & Wigham Richardson Limited and it was from this company that de Havilland acquired the shares.

The newly merged group was given the task of designing a bomber that would be light in weight and lack defensive weaponry, relying on its high-speed capability to achieve its strike objectives. A design that made use of the lightweight techniques used in the construction of the pre-war Comet Racer and the Albatross was conceived and the now famous Mosquito was born. A prototype aircraft was built in great secrecy and taken to Hatfield, where Geoffrey de Havilland junior flew it for the first time on 25th November 1940. The aircraft affectionately became known as the "Wooden Wonder", entering service with the RAF in 1941 and, apart from bombing, it was successfully used for photographic reconnaissance, and day and night fighter variants were also built. Powered by two Rolls-Royce Merlin engines the Mosquito had a level speed of 380mph, a range of 1,200 miles and could carry one 1,000lb bomb and two 500lb bombs. It was claimed that the aircraft was faster than the Spitfire

The workforce of the Wrighton Furniture factory, that once stood in Billet Road, Walthamstow, with the 1,000th wooden body of a de Havilland Mosquito produced at the plant, 8th July 1944.

and could out perform nearly all other aircraft of the day. The beauty of this wooden design meant that much of the aircraft's production could be farmed out to furniture manufacturers across the country. Wrightons in Billet Road, Walthamstow, alone produced over one thousand of these machines.

Frank Whittle (1907-96) had worked on the design of the jet engine during the 1930s but as well as being unable to afford the £5 fee to extend his patent he had also to endure a distinct lack of interest by the Air Ministry for his ideas. However, the Air Ministry's concentration rapidly changed with the outbreak of the Second World War and they finally got behind Whittle's development, even sending an engine to America for examination. On 15th May 1941 a select group of people, including Geoffrey de Havilland and his engine designer Frank Halford, were invited to RAF Cranwell, Lincolnshire to witness the first flight of a tiny Gloster (E28/39) aircraft, powered by a Whittle turbojet engine, which had only 860lb of thrust. The historic flight lasted only seventeen minutes but it was enough to stir the enthusiasm of both Geoffrey de Havilland and Frank Halford. On returning to base, Halford began work on a new jet engine, while the aircraft design team, under Ronald Bishop, started work on an innovative new aircraft.

The Air Ministry had given the Rover Car Company a contract to supply engines for the Gloster Meteor from their plant in Lancashire but initially they encountered technical problems. On 5th March 1943 the Meteor made its first flight, powered by two Halford H.1 engines. The H.1 was further developed and became known as the Goblin. Six months after the flight of the Gloster Meteor, on 29th September, Geoffrey de Havilland junior flew the new DH.100 powered by a Goblin engine. The aircraft became known as the Vampire and went into service with the RAF after the war. Apart from being the first jet fighter to fly across the Atlantic in May 1948 and setting a new world altitude record of 59,446ft (18,119m) it also saw active service in Malaya and was used extensively throughout the Suez campaign.

By the late 1940s, manufacturers in Britain and America were developing aircraft powered by jet engines. As the British aircraft industry would discover to its cost, the American authorities had really grasped the potential of the early sample jet engine sent to them by the Air Ministry and this wartime act would lead to the eventual demise of aircraft production in the UK.

The quest for speed had brought about the proliferation of experimental aircraft designs and it was probably inevitable that disaster would soon strike. Geoffrey de Havilland junior, an experienced test pilot, was killed when his experimental DH.108 aircraft broke up over Kent on 27th September 1946. It was thought that the aircraft was approaching the sound barrier when the failure occurred. On 26th September 1951 the DH.110, piloted by the de Havilland chief test pilot and former wartime fighter pilot ace John Cunningham, made its first test flight and the following year he exceeded the magic Mach 1. At the Farnborough Air Show later that year John Derry and his observer, Tony Richards flying a DH.110 lost their lives as the aircraft broke up, killing 28 spectators and injuring 63 others.

Perhaps the most memorable aircraft to come out of the de Havilland stable at Hatfield was the world's first commercial jet airliner, the Comet. On 27th July 1949 with John Cunningham at the controls, the first prototype, the DH.106, powered by four turbojet engines flew for thirty-one minutes. Later that year the aircraft made its first public appearance at the Farnborough Air Show. After considerable prototype testing, the first production Comet (G-ALYP) received its certificate of airworthiness on 22nd January 1952. On 2nd May that year, less than fifty years after the Wright brother's historic flight, the world's first jet airliner service took off from London in BOAC colours with fare-paying passengers to Johannesburg.

The Comet was an instant hit with the public and its success was further consolidated when Queen Elizabeth the Queen Mother became the first member of the Royal Family to fly in a jet aircraft. However, the early success was short lived, as disaster struck on 10th January 1954 when BOAC Flight 781 crashed into the sea off the Italian island of Elba with the loss of all on board. Then on 8th April a further major tragedy occurred when South African Airways Flight 201 (chartered from BOAC), en route from Rome to Cairo, crashed near Naples. Immediately after this second disastrous event all Comet flights were grounded and engineers began the laborious task of examining the recovered wreckage to methodically piece together the reasons for failure. After what was to become the longest ever programme of flight testing in history it was discovered that failure had occurred due to a then little-understood phenomenon: metal fatigue.

The lessons learned from the crash examinations carried out at Farnborough were incorporated into the new Comet 4 and the results of the findings were made available to all aircraft manufacturers. Although the new version was to fly the first scheduled transatlantic service on 4th October 1958, the delays and loss of confidence from both the public and commercial airlines had sounded the death knell for de Havilland. This situation had probably been compounded by events in the early 1940s when the Air Ministry had sent a sample of Frank Whittle's jet engine to America. This had given aircraft companies like McDonnell Douglas and Boeing the opportunity to study the new technology and incorporate it into their later aircraft designs. Airliners like the DC8 and the 707 became popular with airlines around the world and their greater transatlantic performance began to expose a weakness in the Comet's range.

On 28th April 1960, BOAC took delivery of its first Boeing 707 (G-APFD). The aircraft flew non-stop from Seattle in the USA to London, a distance of 4,900 miles, in 9 hours 44 minutes. It was probably demonstrations like this that made BOAC consider the Comet's future role and by 1964 it had decided to withdraw all its nineteen Comets from service and put them up for sale.

Although the de Havilland Company had produced many successful commercial and military aircraft, the costs of competing internationally were beginning to take their toll. In January 1960, the Hawker Siddeley Group, founded by Sir Thomas Sopwith, was successful in its bid for de Havilland and the group was reorganised. On 1st July 1963 the de Havilland Aircraft Company became a Division of Hawker Siddeley Aviation Limited.

De Havilland Comet 4 (G-APDB), sold to Dan-Air Services Limited in 1969, was the first jet airliner to cross the Atlantic with fare-paying passengers on 4th October 1958.

Geoffrey de Havilland died on 21st May 1965 at the age of seventy-two. He had retired from active involvement in his company ten years earlier. Geoffrey's resting place is where his flying career began as, after cremation, his ashes were scattered over Seven Barrows in Hampshire. During his life he received many honours; the OBE in 1918, the Air Force Cross in 1919, a CBE in 1934 and a knighthood in 1944. In 1962 he was appointed to the Order of Merit.

In July 2002, actress Olivia de Havilland attended the unveiling of a campus of the University of Hertford named in honour of her cousin Geoffrey. The building, which stands on land near where the Hatfield factory once stood, is a fitting memorial to one of our greatest aircraft pioneers who saw his machines evolve from a single crude experiment to sleek jet airliners that circled the world.

REFERENCES

Author unknown, *De Havilland – The Man & The Company*, Royal Air Force Museum, London, 2007.

De Havilland, Geoffrey, *Sky Fever: The Autobiography of Sir Geoffrey de Havilland*, Peter & Anne de Havilland, London, 1961.

Jackson, A.J., *De Havilland Aircraft Since 1909,* Putnam, 1987.

Karwatka, Dennis, *Moving Civilization, The Growth of Transportation*, Prakken Publications, Inc., Kentucky, 2003.

Matthew, H.C.G. and Harrison, Brian, (ed.), *The Oxford Dictionary of National Biography*, Oxford, 2004.

McGovern, Una, (ed.), *Chambers Biographical Dictionary*, Chambers Harrap Publishers Ltd., Edinburgh, 2003.

Smith, Ron, *British Built Aircraft*, Vol.4, Tempus Publishing, Stroud, 2004.

Taylor, J.W.R. *Images of Aviation, the de Havilland Aircraft Company*, Tempus Publishing, 1996.

Note

The Birmingham Small Arms Company (BSA) was established in 1861, after the Crimean War, when a group of gun contractors in the Midlands were forced to come together to set up a business to manufacture a range of standardised small arms with interchangeable parts. This group of contractors had taken the initiative to move from a craft-based industry as the British government had made it abundantly clear that because of changing military requirements they would no longer issue contracts for small arms made by traditional methods.

Interestingly, the industrial changes after the Crimean War, when a surplus of weapons existed, had come about because of the increased need for the standardisation of military small arms. The changes that had come about in the aircraft industry after the Great War were also due to a surplus (in this case of aircraft) with a marked reduction in the military requirement. Therefore, both the post-war conditions, although similar in character, had a quite opposite effect on the two different industries.

8. CARLESS, CAPEL AND LEONARD –
WHAT'S IN A NAME?

In 1859 Eugene Carless, a chemist, set up in business as a distiller and refiner of mineral oils at Hackney Wick, then a small east London hamlet. His timing could not have been better and was to prove a remarkable stroke of luck. By coincidence, in America that year Colonel Edwin L. Drake drilled what was considered to be the first successful oil well at Titusville, Pennsylvania. The event is now regarded as the beginning of the modern petroleum industry.

Carless had secured the lease on a piece of land at Hackney Wick from a local pork butcher and a little later he leased another plot on Old Ford Marsh, along with an adjoining house at 5 White Post Lane. Here, in 1860, Carless constructed the Hope Chemical Works and later that year he joined with the businessman William George Blagden to form the firm of Carless, Blagden & Company. The partnership first concentrated their resources on refining quantities of British shale oil and coal tar, the latter a by-product of the expanding gas industry, from which derived paraffin oil, benzoline and other products. Interestingly, the company had developed a

Eugene Carless

John Hare
Leonard

The Hope Chemical Works, Hackney Wick, the original factory of Carless, Capel & Leonard.

product they called Carburine, a spirit that employed the use of a carburettor (an appliance now used for carburetion of air in petrol engines), a very rare device for the day. In a leaflet produced by the company it was claimed that, "The Carburine and Carburettor as manufactured by Carless, Blagden & Co. are the only means at present known of improving the quality and increasing the illuminating power of common gas advantageously". The leaflet also mentioned that St Paul's church at Stratford had used this method of lighting for *upwards of twelve months*. This would suggest that their carburettor, a mechanism for vaporising or atomising fuel, was in use by 1864, around two years before the generally accepted date of the introduction of this device.

When the partnership dissolved in 1870, Carless turned to refining the newly imported American crude oil and soon became Britain's leading distiller of the product. During the early 1870s, Carless was introduced to George Bligh Capel, a businessman who sank £3,000 into the firm. In April 1872, another businessman, John Hare Leonard, joined the partners and the company was re-named Carless, Capel & Leonard. At about this time Carless seems to have relinquished his partnership and instead took on the role of works manager. It is probable that he was more comfortable with a hands-on role rather than the day-to-day financial and business involvement. Within eighteen months of joining the business, Leonard became sole proprietor although the company name remained unchanged.

The introduction of the Locomotive Act had meant that self-propelled vehicles were restricted to speeds of no more than 2mph

The early Carless, Capel & Leonard transport fleet.

(3.2km/h) in towns and 4mph (6.4km/h) elsewhere. To ensure that these speeds were adhered to, vehicles had to be preceded by a man carrying a red flag. These measures had the effect of keeping mechanically propelled vehicles off the roads and they also stifled the development of the motorcar in Britain. It was not until 1896 that the Act was effectively repealed by the introduction of the Locomotives on Highways Act that allowed speeds in Britain to increase to 12mph (19.2km/h). However, during this time Carless, Capel & Leonard had not remained idle and had improved and developed the production of petroleum oil and petroleum spirit. This had attracted the attention of Frederick Simms who had connections with the motor vehicle pioneer, Gottlieb Daimler. At the time, Daimler was looking for a spirit of high volatility and, as later correspondence between J.H. Leonard's son William and Frederick Simms shows, he got what he wanted.

In essence, the correspondence relates to a discussion between Simms and Leonard in January 1893 over the difficulties of devising a trade name for the petroleum spirit supplied to Daimler. Eventually, Simms got his way and the name Petrol was officially born. Leonard tried to register Petrol as a Trade Mark, but as the law then stood, this was not allowed.

In 1896, Petrol was given a marketing boost when it was used by those taking part in the London to Brighton Run (then known as the Emancipation Run), and that year Carless, Capel & Leonard was presented with the Automobile Club's silver medal for its motor spirit, the only distillers to receive such an award. At the time, Petrol was sold in 10-gallon drums at the price of 11d per gallon, but distribution in those early days, particularly by the railway operators, was not straightforward as these companies considered the product dangerous to transport. To address the nervousness of the railway operators, and as an additional safety measure, the Hackney Wick factory filled four-gallon cans with Petrol and packed them into wooden cases, each containing only two cans. This early arrangement for transporting fuel is a far cry from the juggernaut vehicles that deliver petrol to our filling stations today.

In 1989, after many years of diversification and expansion, Carless, Capel & Leonard was taken over and broken up, leaving little trace of the company's original roots. However, it can not be denied that this was another regional company that, through the foresight and dedication of its founders, was able to add at least two more industrial firsts (Petrol and the development of the carburettor) to the long list of Lea Valley technological achievements.

PETROL.

CARLESS, CAPEL & LEONARD, of Hope Chemical Works, and Pharos Works, Hackney Wick, London, N.E., specially distil Petrol, the Spirit best adapted for Motors, Motor Carriages, Launches, etc., etc.

Maximum of efficiency and perfect combustion; therefore great economy, and no deposit in cylinders.

No Smell,
No Dirt,
No Trouble.

CARLESS, CAPEL & LEONARD have supplied the above for the Daimler Motors for over eight years, and hold the highest testimonials.

They also supply Lubricating Oils and Greases.

SAMPLES AND PRICES ON APPLICATION.

Telegrams: "CARLESS, HACKNEY WICK."

PETROL.

For List of Agents see pages 33 to 43.

An advertisement extolling the virtues of Petrol from a company brochure of 1901.

A Carless tanker leaving the headquarters of ICI Paints Division (c.1960).

REFERENCES

Pugh, Peter, *Carless, Capel & Leonard PLC, The Growth of a Family Firm Into an International Company*, Carless, Capel & Leonard, London, 1986.

The Petroleum Times, 17th June 1949.

9. FROM STEAM ENGINES TO FAMILY CARS – THE STORY OF VAUXHALL MOTORS

Like many other prominent Lea Valley manufacturers, Vauxhall, as the name might suggest to readers familiar with London's districts, began life elsewhere. The origins of the name Vauxhall and the griffin company logo, have their roots in the 13th century. Fulke le Breant, an ambitious mercenary, was granted the Manor of Luton for his services to King John. He was also granted the right to bear arms. For his heraldic identity Fulke adopted the symbol of a griffin. Through marriage to a wealthy widow, Margaret de Redvers, Fulke acquired land and property close to London on the south bank of the River Thames. The property soon became known locally as Fulke's Hall, but later the name became corrupted, first to Foxhall, then to Vaux Hall and eventually to the more familiar Vauxhall.

In the mid seventeenth century, pleasure gardens were established at Vauxhall and were named New Spring Gardens, to avoid confusion with the Old Spring Gardens located at Charing Cross. When Jonathan Tyers assumed management of the Gardens in the eighteenth century he totally transformed them, laying out gravelled paths, a Grand Walk that was 900 feet (274m) long and lined with elm trees and a South Walk that was bridged by three

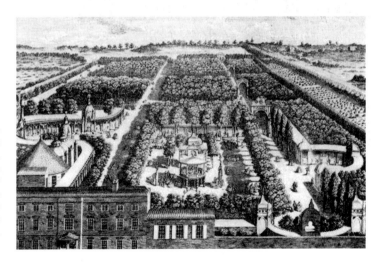

The Vauxhall Pleasure Gardens that were first established in the mid seventeenth century on the south side of the River Thames. To the right of the picture can be seen the Grand Walk, added in the eighteenth century, bridged by triumphal arches.

triumphal arches. After remodelling the only house on site into a footman's waiting room, he then added lavishly decorated supper boxes, some with pictures painted by Hogarth. Near to these an orchestra of fifty musicians was installed. Further additions were a music room and a Chinese Pavilion. A leading sculptor was commissioned to make a statue of Handel and this was erected at the entrance to the gardens. In June 1732 the gardens opened with much pomp and ceremony and visitors were charged one guinea each for admission. After Tyler's death in 1767, the management of the gardens passed to his two sons. In 1785 the name of the gardens was changed to Vauxhall Gardens. By the mid nineteenth century the gardens had lost their former splendour and the visitor numbers had dwindled. They finally closed in July 1859 and the land was eventually used for housing.

In 1857, Alexander Wilson, a Scottish engineer, founded the firm Alexander Wilson & Company in the area close to Vauxhall Gardens. As a company emblem Wilson adopted the Fulke le Breant griffin. Initially the firm manufactured a range of machinery, from pumps to powerful marine steam engines. By 1894 Wilson had left the company he had founded to become an engineering consultant. His leaving seems to have been around the time when the company

A steam engine built at the Vauxhall Ironworks in the late nineteenth century and destined for a twin-paddled steam ship.

A 1903 Vauxhall four-seater with the occupants in the front sitting above the engine. Note the "tiller" type steering column next to the driver at the left of the picture.

had begun experimenting with internal combustion engine technology. After getting into financial difficulties, the company was restructured by the new owners and became the Vauxhall Iron Works Company Limited.

By the late nineteenth century there was a growing interest in the invention of the internal combustion engine, particularly with regard to road transport. When the mandatory speed limit was raised from four to twelve miles per hour in November 1896 the interest increased. In 1897, Vauxhall Ironworks developed its first petrol engine. This was a single-cylinder model and was fitted to a small river launch called the *Jabberwock*. It is thought that the success of this engine provided the enthusiasm for the directors, F.W. Hodges and J.H. Chambers, to take the development a stage further and the company built a 5hp engine. In 1903 this engine powered Vauxhall's first production motorcar. The car, by today's standards, was rather primitive with only two forward speeds and no reverse. There was no steering wheel and a "tiller" type arm on a column was used to manoeuvre the car whilst a hand throttle adjusted the speed. Around 40 two-seat and four-seat models were sold at prices starting at £136.

The following year, encouraged by these early sales, a 6hp version with a reverse gear was designed. The car was entered in the

London to Glasgow reliability trial and in spite of being the smallest entry in the field it was awarded 993 points out of a possible 1,000. Competing in the trial had shown Vauxhall's directors the future and in September 1904 the car's "tiller" was replaced with a steering wheel. With confidence in the motorcar industry growing, the Vauxhall directors tested the market at the end of 1904 with the launch of a 12/14hp model at the higher price of £375.

By early 1905, with the factory lease running out and the need for expansion, the decision was taken to move the company from south London to new premises at Luton, Bedfordshire in the upper Lea Valley. The move took place on 29th March 1905. Interestingly, the company had returned to the place granted to Fulke le Breant by King John almost seven hundred years earlier. Also returning to Luton, with Vauxhall, was le Breant's heraldic symbol of the griffin, which the company would adopt as a vehicle logo.

The first car to be manufactured at Luton, in 1905, was a 7/9hp model that was underpowered for its weight and was later discontinued. For the London Motor Show that year Vauxhall introduced a lightweight 9hp model. A four-cylinder 18hp model was also put on display that was styled with distinctive sculptured flutes either side of the bonnet. This characteristic bodywork feature was to stay with the design of Vauxhall motorcars for over fifty years until 1959.

Early production at Luton. Prior to the First World War, motorcar chassis were assembled on the spot. Flow-line techniques had yet to be introduced.

A Vauxhall on snow-covered roads during the 1912 Swedish Winter Cup Trials.

By 1907 it had become clear to Vauxhall's directors that operating as a general engineering company, making a diverse range of equipment, was a distraction from what was now clearly the future: the motorcar. To this end Vauxhall Motors Limited was established to concentrate on the design, development and manufacture of motor vehicles.

In the winter of 1907 the Royal Automobile Club (RAC) published the rules for their 2,000-mile reliability trial. The trial was scheduled to take place over thirteen days and would include timed hill climbs in Scotland and the Lake District plus a 200-mile speed test at the Brooklands race circuit. As considerable publicity could be gained from performing well in such a high profile event, Vauxhall decided to enter. However, Vauxhall lacked a suitable car to take part and, to make matters worse, their chief engineer was abroad on holiday. A young engineer, Laurence Pomeroy, was given the job of designing a car for the trial. Within a few weeks Pomeroy had come up with a design for a 20hp model and the concept was ready by the time the chief engineer returned.

By June 1908 the car was built and ready. Called the A-type it was driven by Percy Kidner, a Vauxhall director, and amazingly took first place at the RAC Trial, even beating the Rolls-Royce entry. For its time the A-type achieved some remarkable performances. In December 1909, a slim-bodied version, called the KN (after cayenne pepper "Hot Stuff") and driven by A.J. Hancock, a Vauxhall works race competitor, set a record for the flying half-mile at Brooklands of 88.6mph and went on to complete a distance record of ten laps averaging 81.33mph. Perhaps even more startling, in 1910 and again driven by Hancock, the A-type clocked 100.08mph, becoming the first motor vehicle in the world below 21hp to do so. Over the next few years, under Laurence Pomeroy's talented stewardship, new models were introduced and designs improved. Vauxhall competed in various touring and sporting events across Europe, setting more world records and thereby increasing the brand's profile and popularity with the buying public.

By the time of the Great War, the 25hp D-type that started life in 1912 had become a favourite with the British Army, which placed orders for almost 2,000 of these cars. The vehicle was adopted as the standard army staff car and became famed for its reliability. When King George V made his tour of inspection of the battlefields of Flanders, it was in a Vauxhall D-type. The model was finally discontinued in 1921, but not before a further 2,000 were sold.

The inter-war years brought changes to people's lifestyles as Britain began the task of rebuilding the economy after a conflict that had robbed the nation of many young men and therefore much of its skilled workforce. The Great War had also placed a heavy financial drain on the Exchequer. For manufacturers like Vauxhall to survive in this unsettled climate, new strategies would be required and new products would have to be designed. The market for the motorcar, although public interest in ownership was growing, had moved away from large, powerful, high-performance vehicles that were really the preserve of the rich and the specialist towards a mass middle- and working-class market. Now manufacturers faced the challenge of developing more modestly priced affordable vehicles of lower engine capacities.

Vauxhall's first attempt to meet the challenge was in 1922 with the introduction of the M-type, a 14hp car with a price tag of £650. In 1924, probably encouraged by the increasing number of people becoming interested in motorcycles, a decision was taken to test this market. Six prototype motorcycles were built, which for the time incorporated several futuristic features. These included a four-cylinder 998cc engine and a shaft drive. However, it soon became evident that the production of such high specification machines would be too costly for a mass market and the project was abandoned.

The year 1925 marked a significant turning point in Vauxhall's fortunes, when A.P. Sloan Junior, the President of General Motors of

The experimental Vauxhall four-cylinder engine motorcycle with shaft drive and saddle tank, 1924. For its day this machine was in advance of anything yet designed.

America, bought the company for $2,500,000. Luton now became General Motors' first manufacturing base in Europe. With the power and also the designs of such a massive automobile company behind it, Vauxhall now found itself in a much stronger position to attack the evolving British mass-car market. In 1930 the American influence soon became clear with the launch of the 17hp and 26hp versions of the six-cylinder Cadet, the first car in Britain to have a synchromesh gearbox, and coming in below the £300 mark. The introduction of the Cadet signalled the aggressive marketing nature of the new owners, as even with the added feature of synchromesh, the car was less than half the price of the earlier Vauxhall M-type. Following in 1933 were the even more successful 12hp and 14hp versions of the Light Six that sold at £195 and £215 respectively. By the end of the year the Light Six had claimed 40 per cent of the British car market for models below 14hp.

By 1934 the Luton plant was really buzzing; the output of the Light Six topped 20,000 vehicles, annual turnover exceeded £7,000,000 and the workforce had increased to 6,000 employees. In 1935 the new six-cylinder 12hp and 14hp DY and DX models became the first British medium-priced cars to have independent front suspension. Perhaps it was not surprising that the 1935 combined sales for these two models reached 26,000. An up-market 80mph G-type was introduced in 1937, which included such novel features as a built-in heater, fog light, reversing light and hydraulic brakes. In the same year the Vauxhall Ten was introduced, a truly mass-market car that would set the standard in cost-effective production and

A 1931 Bedford 2-ton truck from the first year of production.

assembly techniques, not just for Vauxhall but for other manufacturers. The Ten, selling at £168, was the first British car to have an integral body and chassis. In the first five months of production, 10,000 of these cars were sold and within three years a total of 55,000 had left the Luton factory.

With the start of the Second World War Vauxhall, like many other manufacturing plants, became engaged in war work. It was fortunate that Vauxhall had already established the successful

Workers celebrating the 10,000th pre-war Vauxhall 10 to be manufactured. The car sold for £168 and in three years customers snapped up 55,000 of these models.

A Second World War Churchill tank manufactured at Luton standing next to a production model Ten-Four.

"Bedford" commercial truck plant in 1931, which was to supply the armed forces with a total of 250,000 vehicles throughout the six-year conflict. One of these, the QL, a four-wheel-drive, became the first four-by-four to be produced by the company. Perhaps one of Vauxhall's most outstanding wartime achievements was the design and manufacture of the famous Churchill tank. Only twelve months after the drawing office began the design work, the first of 5,640 Churchills to be built at Luton left the factory. Around the country, ten other factories were contracted to assemble Churchill tanks from parts manufactured at Luton. When the 38-ton Churchill

The Prime Minister Winston Churchill inspecting the tank that was named after him in the grounds of Luton Hoo.

encountered damage on the battlefield the tanks were shipped back to Luton for repair. In all, 3,000 of these monsters were put back into working order with the help of a dedicated workforce.

The 200,000th wartime Bedford truck being driven out of the factory by an army driver.

The manufacture and repair of tanks and trucks was not all that was going on at the Vauxhall plant in aid of the war effort. Apart from top-secret work on jet engines and the development of aircraft for the Royal Air Force, there was the manufacture of 5,000,000 sides for fuel cans, production of 4,000,000 rocket engine components, the design and assembly of decoy trucks and aircraft, the making of some 750,000 helmets and the turning out of up to 5,000 armour-piercing shells per week. With all this work in support of the war it was almost inevitable that the Luton factory would become a target for enemy bombers. In August 1940, the Luftwaffe raided the factory and as a result, thirty-nine Vauxhall workers were killed.

Immediately after the war Vauxhall production was switched back to its traditional base and the first cars to be produced were the pre-war types. However, few of these models reached the British market as the government, in an effort to replenish the Exchequer's depleted coffers, encouraged manufacturers to export their output. By the early 1950s, with the country desperate to leave the years of wartime austerity behind, new fashions in clothes were emerging

Bedford trucks lining
Kimpton Road, Luton during
World War Two,
awaiting collection.

and motorcar bodywork took on a more rounded look. Vauxhall
launched the E-type, which incorporated a full-width body shell
and sculptured front wings with lights. When Vauxhall reached the
Golden Jubilee year in 1953, annual production had topped
100,000 units, the millionth vehicle had left the Luton plant and
the workforce totalled 13,000 employees.

The E-type Vauxhall Wyvern
nearing completion. It was
Vauxhall's first post-war car
with the new full-width body
shell design that incorporated
the front wings and lights.

In 1954, with confidence growing and an increasing public post-
war interest in car ownership, Vauxhall made a massive
commitment to Luton with a £36 million investment to improve
and upgrade production facilities. By the close of the decade the

two millionth car had been built, the annual turnover had risen to a staggering £76 million, the workforce was in the order of 22,000 employees and the distinctive bonnet flute had been styled out after gracing successive models for fifty-nine years.

In the 1960s, to keep up with the public's growing appetite for car ownership, there was a dramatic increase in manufacturing capacity right across the automotive industry. In Britain, manufacturers were encouraged to set-up new factories in special economic development areas. These tended to be located where there were high levels of unemployment in regions like Merseyside. In 1960, Vauxhall began construction of its second manufacturing facility, south of the Mersey, in Ellesmere Port, Cheshire. Completion of this second plant gave Vauxhall the necessary capacity to become a major British producer. Now, with the introduction in 1963 of the Viva, a small family car, the company was able, for the first time, to compete directly with mid-range models produced by Ford, British Leyland and the Rootes Group. For a time the future looked decidedly rosy with the introduction of new model ranges that were popular with the public. Healthy annual sales figures in both the commercial vehicle and family car divisions followed. However, with the approach of the next decade the upbeat progress of the company was about to change.

The launch of the Victor in 1957. At the time, Vauxhall employed 22,000 people and the annual turnover for the company was £76 million.

By the late 1970s, less than twenty years after the automotive industry's massive expansion programme, the effects of overcapacity, market competition and Britain's economic downturn, helped by the Middle East oil crisis, were taking their toll and Vauxhall saw a sharp decline in sales. Nevertheless, General Motors had the confidence and vision to believe that the market would eventually turn and, in the early 1980s, backed their instincts with the announcement of a massive cash injection of £100 million. The cash was to improve production facilities at Ellesmere Port and £90 million of the sum was earmarked to construct a new paint plant at Luton. With the introduction of later versions of the popular Cavalier, a first-time entry into the small car market with the Nova and, in 1984, the launch of the all-new Astra, car sales passed the 300,000 mark in 1985 for the first time in the company's history. There was also good news for market share, which reached a post-war record of almost 23 per cent. By 1987, Vauxhall had turned in a £31 million net profit in contrast to a £118 million loss sustained for the preceding three years. The year also saw the largest single order for Vauxhall cars when Thorn EMI took delivery of 20,000 cars. In 1989 registrations of Vauxhall cars reached an all-time high of almost 350,000 units and the company achieved record profits for the third consecutive year.

In 1986, the former Lea Valley high performance car company Lotus, founded by Colin Chapman, became part of the General Motors empire. The amalgamation brought about, in 1990, the launch of the highest performance car ever manufactured by Vauxhall, the Lotus Carlton. Also in this year Vauxhall's new corporate headquarters, Griffin House, Osborne Road, Luton was opened. The style and scale of the building reflected an air of confidence in Luton's permanence. Despite falling industry sales, Vauxhall, during the 1990s, pressed ahead with the introduction of new models like the off-road Frontera and also with a massive investment in Ellesmere Port of £193 million to build the ECOTEC V6 engine plant. A further £136 million was injected at Luton to completely modernise the factory, which included the installation of four hundred state-of-the-art robotic welding and handling systems.

December 1996 saw the signing of an agreement between Vauxhall, IBC Vehicles (a company originally formed in 1987 by General Motors and Isuzu of Japan), General Motors and Renault to develop and manufacture a new range of medium-sized vans at Luton. The plant that would carry out this joint venture was established next to the Vauxhall car factory. In 1998 General Motors took control of the IBC Vehicles side of the partnership by buying out Isuzu and the company now trades under the name of GMM Luton. By 2005 the joint venture was turning out in excess of 90,000 vehicles per year with a local workforce of 1,900 employees working a twenty-four hour, three-shift system. Some of the names of the commercial vehicles produced will no doubt be familiar to the reader: Vauxhall Arena, Opel Vivaro, Renault Trafic and Nissan Primastar.

As the new millennium dawned the car industry across the world suffered the effects of overcapacity as the last decades of the old century had seen increasing competition from Eastern European and Far Eastern manufacturers. General Motors, the world's largest producer, with manufacturing and distribution sites across the globe, was haemorrhaging dollars. To address the situation the company put in place a massive global restructuring plan, which inevitably translated into cutbacks and job losses. In March 2002, after ninety-seven years at the site, Vauxhall produced her 7,415,045th car, the last to be made at Luton.

Modern-day automobile manufacturing, compared to that of the 1970s and 1980s, would be almost unrecognisable to those who had earlier worked in the industry. Robotics and computer-controlled machinery have replaced many skilled engineering jobs and the system of just in time (JIT) material delivery with computerised storage and recovery systems have further reduced

A display of Vauxhall motorcars from the vintage collection.

the workforce. With sophisticated computerised communication systems it is possible for software to control machinery, update component handling and modify vehicle design. Information can be sent via satellite to a company's production sites anywhere in the world and what we are witnessing is the natural evolution of technological innovation.

However, in spite of the rationalisation of car manufacturing at Luton, the region has benefited from further investment by General Motors. In May 2000 the opening of the new Vauxhall Engineering Centre at Millbrook, Bedfordshire brought vehicle research and development back to the UK. The following year, in April, a new Pan-European, multi-lingual Customer Care Centre, serving twenty countries, was opened at Luton. Further prosperity was brought to the Luton commercial vehicle plant with a joint investment of £430 million by Renault and General Motors to manufacture the Vivaro range of vans. The year 2005 marked one hundred years of continuous vehicle manufacture at Luton. There are few places in Britain that can claim such a remarkable achievement.

REFERENCES

Author unknown, *The Vauxhall Story*, Vauxhall Education Service, Luton, 2001.

Burgess-Wise, David, *A Centenary in Motion 1903 – 2003*, CW Publishing, Oxford, 2003.

Duerden, Andrew, Vauxhall heritage, a personal conversation, October 2007.

Scott, W.S., *History of Kennington and its Neighbourhood*, London, 1899.

Montgomery, H.H., *Green Retreats: The Story of Vauxhall Gardens 1661-1859*.

APPENDIX: THE THAMES IRONWORKS AND THE WORLD'S HIGHEST NAVIGABLE WATERWAY

While holidaying in Peru in September 2008 the author was fortunate to uncover the little-known story of the *Yavari*, a mid-nineteenth-century boat that was built in Britain and is now afloat on Lake Titicaca at a height of 12,500 feet (3,810m) in the Andes Mountain range.

In May 1861, the Peruvian Navy placed an order for a boat of three hundred tons with the British agents, Anthony Gibbs & Sons. Admiral Mariscal Ramon Castilla was sent to Britain to commission a shipyard to build the vessel for a new base to be established on Lake Titicaca and also vessels for other Peruvian bases. Castilla had an unusual request for the shipyard that he would ultimately appoint to build the *Yavari*. The boat would have to be designed in such a way that it could be carried by mules.

A picture of a mule train similar to the one that would have carried the sections of the *SS Yavari* across the Andes mountain range. However, the *SS Yavari* mule train would have consisted of around one hundred mules.

A healthy mule could carry only between three and four hundred-weight (170kg). This would mean that the boat would have to be manufactured in the form of a prefabricated kit. It would also have to be crated and shipped to Peru, where individual pieces would be strapped on mules to be led by porters up the perilous tracks of the Andes Mountain range from sea-level to Lake Titicaca, the highest navigable waterway in the world. Castilla soon learned that it would not be possible for a boat of three hundred tons to be broken down for easy transportation by mules and a compromise was reached by changing the order to two gun boats weighing one hundred and forty tons each.

The famous James Watt Foundry in Birmingham was commissioned to build the boats and they in turn sub-contracted the manufacture of the iron

hulls to the Thames Ironworks & Shipbuilding Company, at Canning Town in London. James Watt signed the letter of contract to build the *Yavari* and her sister ship, the *Yapura*, on 10th October 1861. On completion (the boats had been assembled to ensure everything fitted together correctly) they were stripped down into two kits, each containing 2,766 pieces, which were then numbered and marked appropriately in red and green to identify the port and starboard sides. After crating, the kits were shipped from London Docks on 28th June 1862 arriving in Arica, Peru on 15th October where the cargo was offloaded and placed in a warehouse for safe keeping, there to await the next phase of the operation.

In May 1863 a naval officer, Commander Ignacio Duenas, was sent to the docks at Arica to supervise the next stage of the kit's movements and the sensible decision was made to send one boat up the Andes at a time. Tenders were issued, in June, inviting contractors to bid for the mammoth task of transporting 2,766 components including steam boiler parts, iron plates, crankshafts, timber, tools, jacks, and sacks of rivets. In September 1863 the *Yavari* kit was weighed and loaded into nine railway carriages then the consignment was taken by steam train thirty-seven miles to the town of Tacna. From there it would travel the remaining one hundred and ninety miles to Puno on Lake Titicaca by mule train.

A team of eight British engineers accompanied the load and when the consignment reached Tacna it was unpacked and the components arranged in the order in which they would be required for assembly. This would hopefully ensure that the boat would be reconstructed in the shortest possible time. The leader of the team, William Partridge, confidently estimated that with a further three qualified engineers he could complete the assembly of the *Yavari* within six months. It was then that Partridge discovered his first major setback when he learned that all the drawings, including the boat's parts list, had been lost somewhere in transit. This was the start of a long line of major difficulties which, unbeknown to him at the time, would take six years to resolve.

Ignoring their first major setback, Partridge and Commander Duenas felt confident that all the other arrangements were now in place, as the mule train contractor had predicted that he could deliver the parts to Lake Titicaca within six months. With six of the engineers (one was left behind to oversee the handing over of the consignment of parts to the mule train contractor) Partridge and Duenas set off on horseback to ride the one hundred and ninety miles, a journey that would take nine days, to Puno. There they would hire local labour and then begin the necessary task of

The *SS Yavari* built for the Peruvian Navy in 1862 at the Thames Ironworks, Canning Town, east London.

building the workshops, jetty and slipway ahead of the full consignment of *Yavari*'s parts arriving. On or after the journey, George Blaxland, a boilermaker, became ill, said to be due to a pulmonary condition; he sadly died some three months after arrival. It might be fair to conclude that in Victorian times such illnesses as altitude sickness were not fully understood and in the spirit of the times, men just stubbornly pushed ahead under the most extreme conditions, perhaps with patriotic loyalties to Queen and country.

The third major setback for the project began when the mule train contractor failed to deliver the parts on time and was promptly sacked. His replacement fared no better. Contractors probably had difficulty in recruiting acclimatised porters and muleteers, and therefore took on people who were accustomed to working at low altitudes. Many of these men abandoned their charges as the climb became too arduous and the carefully planned component delivery sequence became strewn along the mule tracks of the Andes.

To make matters worse, while bits of the *Yavari* were lying across

The replacement Bolinder four-cylinder hot-bulb semi-diesel engine that was fitted in 1914.

the mountains, Peru became involved in a territorial dispute with her long time antagonist and ex-colonial master, Spain. Four twenty-four-pounder Armstrong guns, that were the intended armaments for the two boats and part of the kits, were requisitioned by the military to defend the country.

Finally, on 25th December 1870 at 3pm, after being blessed by a Bishop, the *Yavari* slid into the waters of Lake Titicaca. Apart from a number of internal fitting problems, which had yet to be completed, the authorities had not been able to find a sufficient quantity of good quality coal, from a local source, for the *Yavari*'s boilers. So the next best fuel, which was in plentiful supply, was employed: dried llama dung. For the next forty-three years the Peruvian llama provided the motive force that powered the boat.

Looking towards the stern of the *SS Yavari* from the upper deck.

Over the years the *Yavari* saw various changes of owner. Finally, in 1977, the boat became once more the property of the Peruvian Navy and was renamed *Chucuito*. Many of the boat's original fixtures and fittings were removed to a local museum and the vessel became a place of detention for sailors of the Peruvian Navy. By 1983 the boat was in a sorry state of repair, but fortunately she was discovered by a Meriel Larken. Believing the boat to have been built by Yarrows, which her grandfather, Sir Alfred Yarrow, had owned, she commissioned a Lloyds Condition Survey. The surveyor's report was encouraging, pointing out that the fresh water of the lake, where the boat had remained all her life, and the rarity of the air had helped preserve the ironwork of the hull in excellent condition.

By 1987 Ms Larken had arranged sponsors, formed a registered charity and purchased the boat from the Peruvian Navy. After many

years of hard work, fundraising and enlisting volunteers, in 1998 the *Yavari* was officially opened as a State Registered Museum (RDN No. 348 INC) by the British Ambassador His Excellency Mr John Illman.

While this is a great story of Victorian engineering and sacrifice, it is also a story of one person's tenacity to restore and preserve a piece of engineering heritage for the benefit of future generations.

The *SS Yavari*'s sister ship, the *SS Yapura*, also built at the Thames Ironworks. Both vessels are berthed on Lake Titicaca at a height of 12,500 feet in the Andes mountain range, South America.

REFERENCES

Larken, Meriel, *1862: Vapor Yavari, Navigation on Lake Titicaca*, Peru, Asociacion Peruano Britanica, 2006.

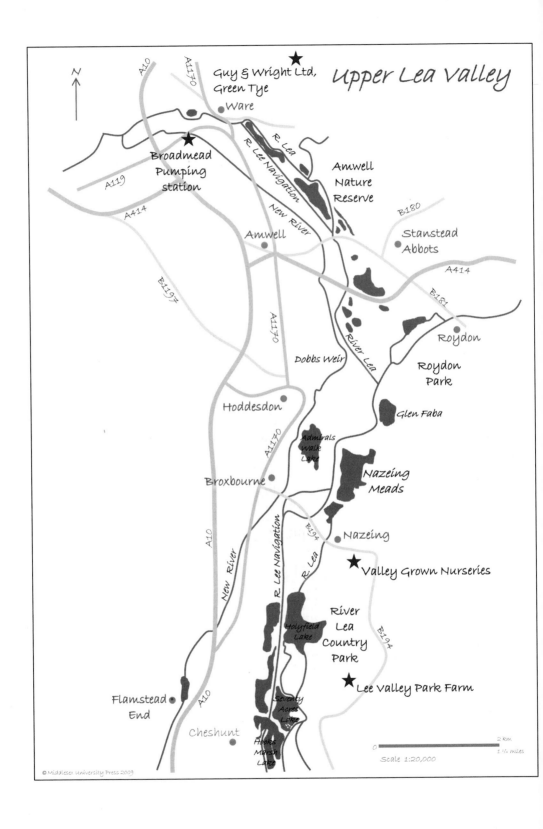

Upper Lea Valley

N

A10
A1170
Guy & Wright Ltd, Green Tye
Ware
R. Lea
R. Lee Navigation
Amwell Nature Reserve
B180
Broadmead Pumping station
A119
New River
Stanstead Abbots
A414
A414
B1197
Amwell
B181
River Lea
Roydon
A1170
Dobbs Weir
Roydon Park
Hoddesdon
Glen Faba
A1170
Admirals Walk Lake
Nazeing Meads
Broxbourne
A10
B194
Nazeing
New River
R. Lee Navigation
R. Lea
Valley Grown Nurseries
Holyfield Lake
River Lea Country Park
B194
Flamstead End
A10
Lee Valley Park Farm
Seventy Acres Lake
Cheshunt
Fishers Marsh Lake

0   2 km
1 ¼ miles
Scale 1:20,000

© Middlesex University Press 2009

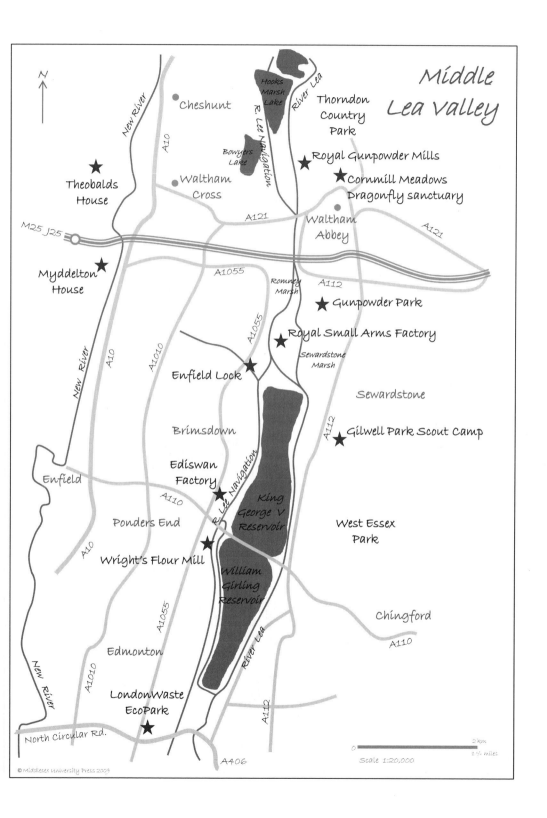

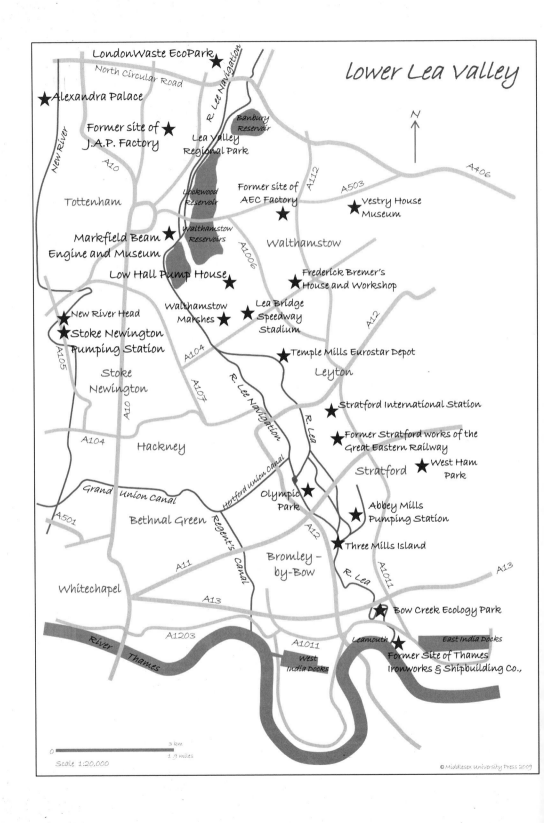

Lower Lea Valley

LondonWaste EcoPark ★

North Circular Road

R. Lee Navigation

★ Alexandra Palace

Former site of ★
J.A.P. Factory

Banbury
Reservoir

Lea Valley
Regional Park

A112

A503

A406

New River

A10

Lockwood
Reservoir

Former site of
AEC Factory
★

★ Vestry House
Museum

Tottenham

Markfield Beam ★
Engine and Museum

Walthamstow
Reservoirs

A1006

Walthamstow

Low Hall Pump House ★

Frederick Bremer's
★ House and Workshop

★ New River Head

Walthamstow
Marshes ★

Lea Bridge
★ Speedway
Stadium

A12

★ Stoke Newington
Pumping Station

A105

A104

A107

R. Lee Navigation

R. Lea

Temple Mills Eurostar Depot
★

Stoke
Newington

A10

Leyton

★ Stratford International Station

Hackney

A104

Grand Union Canal

Hertford Union Canal

Olympic
Park ★

★ Former Stratford Works of the
Great Eastern Railway

Stratford

★ West Ham
Park

A501

Bethnal Green

Regent's Canal

Abbey Mills
★ Pumping Station

A12

★ Three Mills Island

A11

Bromley –
by-Bow

R. Lea

A1011

A13

Whitechapel

A13

A1203

A1011

Leamouth

★ Bow Creek Ecology Park

East India Docks

River Thames

West
India Docks

★
Former Site of Thames
Ironworks & Shipbuilding Co.,

0   3 km
1.9 miles

Scale 1:20,000

© Middlesex University Press 2009